GO TO HEAVEN

FULTON J. SHEEN

GO TO HEAVEN

A Spiritual Road Map to Eternity

IGNATIUS PRESS   SAN FRANCISCO

Dedicated to the LADY who looked down to Heaven
As she held Heaven in her arms

CONTENTS

GO TO HEAVEN

If Horace Greeley had not believed there was such a thing as territory beyond the Mississippi, he would never have said: "Go west, young man." If the modern man did not believe there was such a thing as hell, he would never give so many directives to those to whom he did not like to go there. Nobody ever says: "Go to heaven." That is why we propose in this book to reverse the direction. As a matter of fact, neither hell nor heaven is related to our lives as arbitrary punishments or rewards.

Hell is not related to an evil life, as is generally supposed, as a spanking is related to an act of disobedience, for a spanking need not necessarily follow disobedience, and rarely does in juvenile circles. Rather, hell is related to an evil life as blindness is related to the plucking out of an eye. Heaven is not related to a good life as a medal is related to a school examination; it is rather related to a good life as knowledge to study. By the mere fact that we apply ourselves intellectually, we become learned.

This book is a road map to heaven and follows a very definite pattern. Many of the ideas contained herein have appeared in our previous writings, but they are here ordered in the forms of steps to the Kingdom of Light. The book opens with the story of man full of certain tensions and complexes originating from the conflict between what he ought to do and what he actually does. Once man recognizes that he cannot escape this civil war within by lifting himself by his own psychological bootstraps, he sees that supra-human aid is possible. There is a Truth beyond the reach of his mind and a Power beyond his tepid and weak will. This Truth and this Power are gifts. Man's quest for God, however dim it is, is seen to be answered by God's quest for man.

Once there is this divine romance between divinity and mankind in the person of Christ, there arises the great question confronting every man: Will he appropriate to himself this Divine Life, which is gratis and, therefore, called "grace", or will he reject it?

Life is a tremendous drama in which one may say, "Aye" or "Nay" to his eternal destiny. To admit light to the eye, music to the ear, and food to the stomach is to perfect each of these organs; so too, to admit Truth to the mind and Power to the will is to make us more than a creature, namely, a partaker of the Divine Nature.

From that point on, the signposts to Heaven are clearly marked in succeeding chapters. Some say we have our hell on this earth. We do. We can start it here, but it does not finish here. But heaven has its beginnings here in a true peace of mind in union with Divine Life, but it does not finish here either. That is why we offer the encouragement: "Go to Heaven."

I

The First Faint Summons to Heaven

Men of other generations went to God from the order in the universe; the modern man goes to God through the disorder in himself. The modern soul no longer looks to find God in nature. In other generations, man, gazing out on the vastness of creation, the beauty of the skies, and the order of the planets, deduced the power, the beauty, and the wisdom of the God Who created and sustained that world. But the modern man, unfortunately, is cut off from that approach by several obstacles: he is impressed less with the order of nature than he is with the disorder of his own mind; the atomic bomb has destroyed his awe of nature; and, finally, the science of nature is too impersonal for this self-centered creature. It is the human personality, not nature, which really interests and troubles men today.

This change in our times does not mean that the modern soul has given up the search for God, but only that it has abandoned the more rational, and even more normal, way of finding Him. Not the order in the cosmos, but the disorder in himself; not the visible things of the world, but the invisible frustrations, complexes, and anxieties of his own personality—these are the modern man's starting point when he turns questioningly toward religion. In happier days, philosophers discussed the problem of man; now they discuss man as a problem.

Formerly, man lived in a three-dimensional universe where, from an earth he inhabited with his neighbors, he looked forth to heaven above and to hell below. Forgetting God, man's vision has lately been reduced to a single dimension; namely, that of his own mind.

Where can the soul go, now that a roadblock has been thrown up against every external outlet? Like a city which has had all its outer ramparts seized, man must retreat inside himself. As a body of water that is blocked turns back upon itself, collecting scum, refuse, and silt, so the modern soul (which has none of the goals or channels of the Christian) backs upon itself and in that choked condition collects all the subrational, instinctive, dark, unconscious sediment which would never have accumulated had there been the normal exits of normal times. Man now finds that he is locked up within himself, his own prisoner. Jailed by self, he now attempts to compensate for the loss of the three-dimensional universe of faith by analyzing his mind.

The complexes, anxieties, and fears of the modern soul did not exist to such an extent in previous generations because they were shaken off and integrated in the great social-spiritual organism of Christian civilization. They are, however, so much a part of modern man that one would think they were tattooed on him. Whatever his condition, the modern man must be brought back to God and happiness. If the modern man wants to go to God from the devil, why, then, we will even start with the devil: that is where the Divine Lord began with Magdalen, and He told His followers that, with prayer and fasting, they too could start their evangelical work there.

There is no difference except that of terminology between the frustrated soul of today and the frustrated souls found in the Gospel. The modern man is characterized by three alienations: he is divided from himself, from his fellow man, and from his God. These are the same three characteristics of the frustrated youth in the land of the Gerasenes.

The first of these is self-estrangement. The modern man is no longer a unity, but a confused bundle of complexes and nerves. He is so dissociated, so alienated from himself that he sees himself less as a personality than as a battlefield where a civil war rages between a thousand and one conflicting loyalties. There is no single over-all purpose in his life. His soul is comparable to a menagerie in which a number of beasts, each seeking its own prey, turn one upon the other. Or he may be likened to a radio that is tuned in to several stations; instead of getting any one clearly, it receives only an annoying static.

If the frustrated soul is educated, it has a smattering of uncorrelated bits of information with no unifying philosophy. Then the frustrated soul may say to itself: "I sometimes think there are two of me—a living soul and a Ph.D." Such a man projects his own mental confusion to the outside world and concludes that, since he knows no truth, nobody can know it. His own skepticism (which he universalizes into a philosophy of life) throws him back more and more upon those powers lurking in the dark, dank caverns of his unconsciousness. He changes his philosophy as he changes his clothes. On Monday, he lays down the tracks of materialism; on Tuesday, he reads a best seller, pulls up the old tracks, and lays the new tracks of an idealist; on Wednesday, his new roadway is communistic; on Thursday, the new rails of liberalism are laid; on Friday, he hears a broadcast and decides to travel on Freudian tracks; on Saturday, he takes a long drink to forget his railroading, and on Sunday, ponders why people are so foolish as to go to church. Each day he has a new idol, each week a new mood. His authority is public opinion; when that shifts, his frustrated soul shifts with it. There is no fixed ideal, no great passion, but only a cold indifference to the rest of the world. Because he lives in a continual state of self-reference, his conversational "I's" come closer and closer, as he finds all neighbors increasingly boring if they insist on talking about themselves instead of about him.

The second characteristic of modern man is his isolation from his fellow men. This characteristic is revealed not only by the two world wars in twenty-one years and a constant threat of a third; not only by the growth of class conflict and selfishness wherein each man seeks his own; but also by man's break with tradition and the accumulated heritage of the centuries. Any respect for that tradition is called "reactionary", with the result that the modern soul has developed a commentator mentality which judges yesterday by today, and today by tomorrow. Nothing is more tragic in an individual who once was wise than to lose his memory, and nothing is more tragic to a civilization than the loss of its tradition. The modern soul which cannot live with itself cannot live with its fellow men. A man who is not at peace with himself will not be at peace with his brother. World wars are nothing but macrocosmic signs of the psychic wars waging inside microcosmic muddled souls. If there had not already been battles in millions of hearts, there would be none on the battlefields of the world.

Given a soul alienated from self, lawlessness follows. A soul with a fight inside itself will soon have a fight outside itself with others. Once a man ceases to be of service to his neighbor, he begins to be a burden to him; it is only a step from refusing to live *with* others to refusing to live *for* others. When Adam sinned, he accused Eve, and when Cain murdered Abel, he asked the antisocial question,

"Am I my brother's keeper?" (Gen 4:9). When Peter sinned, he went out *alone* and wept bitterly. Babel's sin of pride ended in a confusion of tongues which made it impossible to maintain fellowship.

Finally, modern man is estranged from God. Alienation from self and from one's fellow men has its roots in separation from God. Once the hub of the wheel, which is God, is lost, the spokes, which are men, fall apart. God seems very far away from the modern man: this is due, to a great extent, to his own Godless behavior. Goodness always appears as a reproach to those who are not living right, and this reproach on the part of the sinner expresses itself in hatred and persecution. There is rarely a disrupted, frustrated soul, critical and envious of his neighbor, who is not at the same time an antireligious man.

The organized atheism of the present hour is thus a projection of self-hatred; no man hates God without first hating himself. Persecution of religion is a sign of the indefensibility of the antireligious or atheistic attitude, for by the violence of hate it hopes to escape the irrationality of Godlessness. The final form of this hatred of religion is a wish to defy God and to maintain one's own evil in the face of His goodness and power. Revolting against the whole of existence, such a soul thinks that it has disproved it; it begins to admire its own torment as a protest against life. Such a soul will not hear about religion, lest the comfort become a condemnation of its own arrogance; it defies it instead. Never able to make sense of its own life, it universalizes its own inner discord and sees the world as a kind of chaos in the face of which it develops the philosophy of "living dangerously".

Does such a confused soul exist in the Gospel? Is modern psychology studying a different type of man from the one Our Divine Lord came to redeem? If we turn to St.

Mark, we find that a young man in the land of the Gerasenes is described as having exactly the same three frustrations as the modern soul.

He was self-estranged, for when Our Lord asked,
"What is thy name?" the young man answered, "My name
is Legion, for we are many" (Mk 5:9). Notice the personality conflict and the confusion between "my" and "we
are many". It is obvious that he is a problem to himself, a
bewildered backwash of a thousand and one conflicting
anxieties. For that reason he called himself "Legion". No
divided personality is happy. The Gospel describes this
unhappiness by saying that the young man was "crying
and cutting himself with stones" (Mk 5:5). The confused
man is always sad; he is his own worst enemy, as he abuses
the purpose of nature for his own destruction.

The young man was also separated from his fellow men,
for the Gospel describes him thus: ". . . And he was always
day and night in the tombs and in the mountains" (Mk
5:5). "He was a menace to other men. . . . For he had been
bound with fetters and chains, and he had rent the chains
asunder and broken the fetters into pieces. And no one
was able to control him . . ." (Mk 5:4, 5). Isolation is a
peculiar quality of Godlessness, whose natural habitat is
away from fellow men, among the tombs, in the region of
death. There is no cement in sin; its nature is centrifugal,
divisive, and disruptive.

He was separated from God, for when he saw the Divine
Savior, he shouted, "What have I to do with Thee, Jesus
the Son of the most high God? I adjure Thee by God that
Thou torment me not" (Mk 5:7). That is to say, "What
have we in common? Your presence is my destruction." It
is an interesting psychological fact that the frustrated soul
hates goodness and wants to be separated from it. Every
sinner hides from God. The very first murderer said, "And

I shall be hidden from thy face, and I shall be a vagabond and a fugitive on the earth" (Gen 4:14).

The important question, then, is not, What will *become* of us, but What will we *be*? The atomic bomb has taken our minds off existence and purpose. Yet it is still true today that how one gets *out* of time is not so important as how one *is* in eternity. The atomic bomb in the hands of a Francis of Assisi would be less harmful than a pistol in the hand of a thug; what makes the bomb dangerous is not the energy it contains, but the man who uses it. Therefore, it is modern man who has to be remade. Unless he can stop the explosions inside his own mind, he will probably— armed with the bomb—do harm to the planet itself, as Pius XII has warned. Modern man has locked himself in the prison of his own mind, and only God can let him out, as He let Peter out of his dungeon. All that man himself must do is to contribute the desire to get out. God will not fail; it is only our human desire that is weak. There is no reason for discouragement. It was the bleating lamb in the thickets, more than the flock in the peaceful pastures, which attracted the Savior's heart and helping hand. But the recovery of peace through His grace implies an understanding of anxiety, the grave complaint of imprisoned modern man.

Modern anxiety is different from the anxiety of previous and more normal ages in two ways. In other days men were anxious about their souls, but modern anxiety is principally concerned with the body; the major worries of today are economic security, health, the complexion, wealth, social prestige, and sex. To read modern advertisements, one would think that the greatest calamity that could befall a person would be to have dishpan hands or a cough in the T-zone. This overemphasis on corporal security is not healthy; it has begotten a generation that is much more concerned about having life jackets to wear on a sea journey than about the cabin it will occupy and enjoy.

The second characteristic of modern anxiety is that it is not a fear of *objective*, natural dangers, such as lightning, beasts, famine; it is *subjective*, a vague fear of what one believes would be dangerous if it happened. That is why it is so difficult to deal with people who have today's types of anxieties; it does no good to tell them that there is no outside danger, because the danger that they fear is inside of them and therefore is abnormally real to them.

It is important to inquire into the basic reason and ground of anxiety, according to man's present historical condition, of which the psychological is only one superficial manifestation. The philosophy of anxiety looks to the fact that man is a fallen being composed of body and soul. Standing midway between the animal and the angel, living in a finite world and aspiring toward the infinite, moving in time and seeking the eternal, he is pulled at one moment toward the pleasures of the body and at another moment to the joys of the spirit. He is in a constant state of suspension between matter and spirit and may be likened to a mountain climber who aspires to the great peak above and yet, looking back from his present position, fears falling to the abyss below. This state of indeterminacy and tension between what he ought to be and what he actually is, this pull between his capacity for enjoyment and its tawdry realization, this consciousness of distance between his yearning for abiding love without satiety and his particular loves with their intermittent sense of "fed-up-ness", this wavering between sacrificing lesser values to attain higher ideals or else abdicating the higher ideals entirely, this pull of the old Adam and the beautiful attraction of the new Adam, this necessity of choice which offers him two roads, one leading to God and the other away from Him—all this makes man anxious about his destiny beyond the stars and fearful of his fall to the depths beneath.

In every man, there is a double law of gravitation, one pulling him to the earth, where he has his time of trial, and the other pulling him to God, where he has his happiness. The anxiety underlying all modern man's anxieties arises from his trying to be himself without God or from his trying to get beyond himself without God. The example of the mountain climber is not exact, for such a man has no helper on the upper peak to which he aspires. Man, however, has a helper—God on the upper peak of eternity reaches out His omnipotent hand to lift him up, even before man raises his voice in plea. It is evident that, even though we escaped all the anxieties of modern economic life, even though we avoided all the tensions which psychology finds in the unconsciousness and consciousness, we should still have that great basic fundamental anxiety born of our creatureliness. Anxiety stems fundamentally from irregulated desires, from the creature wanting something that is unnecessary for him or contrary to his nature or positively harmful to his soul. Anxiety increases in direct ratio and proportion as man departs from God. Every man in the world has an anxiety complex because he has the capacity to be either saint or sinner.

When we see a monkey acting foolishly, we do not say to the monkey, "Do not act like a nut"; but when we see a man acting foolishly, we do say, "Do not act like a monkey." Because a man is spirit, as well as matter, he can descend to the level of beasts (though not so completely as to destroy the image of God in his soul). It is this possibility that makes the peculiar tragedy of man. Cows have no psychoses, and pigs have no neuroses, and chickens are not frustrated (unless these frustrations are artificially produced by man); neither would man be frustrated or have an anxiety complex if he were an animal made *only for this world.*

Since the basic cause of man's anxiety is the possibility of being either a saint or a sinner, it follows that there are only two alternatives for him. Man can either mount upward to the peak of eternity or else slip backward to the chasms of despair and frustration. Yet there are many who think there is yet another alternative, namely, that of indifference. They think that, just as bears hibernate for a season in a state of suspended animation, so they, too, can sleep through life without choosing to live for God or against Him. But hibernation is no escape; winter ends, and one is then forced to make a decision—indeed, the very choice of indifference itself is a decision. White fences do not remain white fences by having nothing done to them; they soon become black fences. Since there is a tendency in us that pulls us back to the animal, the mere fact that we do not resist it operates to our own destruction. Just as life is the sum of the forces that resist death, so, too, man's will must be the sum of the forces that resist frustration. A man who has taken poison into his system can ignore the antidote, or he can throw it out of the window; it makes no difference which he does, for death is already on the march. St. Paul warns us, "How shall we escape if we neglect ...?" (Heb 2:3). By the mere fact that we do not go forward, we go backward. There are no plains in the spiritual life; we are either going uphill or coming down. Furthermore the pose of indifference is only intellectual. The will *must* choose. And even though an "indifferent" soul does not positively reject the infinite, the infinite rejects it. The talents that are unused are taken away, and the Scriptures tell us that, "But because thou art lukewarm, and neither cold nor hot, I will begin to vomit thee out of my mouth" (Rev 3:16).

The Christian is always bound to have a great advantage over the indifferent modern pagan, simply because he knows where he is going, whereas the modern pagan knows nothing. The pagan must always be the pessimist, for he must always feel that this life is too short to give a man a chance, and the Christian will always be the optimist, for he knows that this life is long enough to give a man a chance for eternity. That is why the Christian can be joyful. That is why the pagan is sad and depressed.

The modern mind dislikes the monotony of a life that is consecrated to a single purpose and a final end, and to escape it, often with his own hand, man shuffles off this mortal coil. This positive distaste for repetition so characteristic of our day alone explains the new, the constant demand for new thrills, new excitements, new psychologies, new religions, new morals, new gods, new everything to arouse the already jaded sensibilities and the soul weighted down with world ennui. Instead of saying that those who are full of life hate monotony, we should say that those who are full of life find a positive thrill in monotony. To prove this point one can appeal to those who are essentially full of life and who, therefore, enjoy the thrill of monotony: namely, a child, God, and His Incarnate Son—Our Blessed Savior. There is necessarily bound to be a thrill in working toward any goal or fixed purpose, and therein is the final reason for the romance of repetition. There, too, is the line of division between genuine Christianity and modern paganism. The Christian finds a thrill in repetition because he has a fixed goal; the modern pagan finds repetition monotonous because he has never decided for himself the purpose of living.

The Christian has fixed his goal, namely, to make his life more and more Christ-like. His own nature is like a block of marble, and his will is the chisel. He looks out upon his model, Christ, and with the sharp points of his mortifying chisel, cuts away from his nature great huge chunks of cold selfishness, and then by finer and more delicate touches makes the great model appear forthwith, until finally only the brush of a hand is needed to give it its polished finish. There is no man living who has this Christian ideal who believes that repeated acts of faith, hope and charity, prudence, justice, fortitude, and love are tainted with what the modern mind would call monotony. Each new conquest of self is a new thrill, for each repeated act brings closer and closer that love we fall just short of in all love, eternal union with Our Lord and Savior.

Sometimes, of course, it is not always easy to see just how much progress we are making toward our goal, but though we never see the progress, we never lose sight of the goal. Then we are very much like the tapestry workers, who work not from the front of the tapestry, but always from the rear, keeping ever before their eyes the model of the work to be achieved. They go on drawing thread after thread in a monotonous but thrilling way, never destined to see their completed work until the last thread has been drawn, and the tapestry is turned about to show them how well and how truly they have labored.

Picture a child with a ball, and suppose that he is told that it is the only ball he will ever have to play with. The natural psychological reaction of the child will be to be fearful of playing too much with it, or bouncing it too often, or even pricking it full of pin holes, because he will never have another ball. But suppose that the child is told that perhaps next month, perhaps next week, perhaps even in five minutes, he will be given another ball, which will never wear out, which will always give joy and with which he will never tire of playing. The natural reaction of the child will be to take the first ball a little less seriously, and to begin playing with it joyously and happily, not even caring if someone does prick it full of pin holes, because he is very soon going to have another ball which will endure eternally.

The child with one ball is the modern pagan who has only one ball in the sense that he has one sphere, one world, one life, one earth. He cannot enjoy the earth as much as he would like because he must always be fearful of the earth being taken away from him. He can never even tolerate that any suffering or pain should ever come to his little ball, the earth, for it is the only ball that he will ever have to play with. The Christian, on the other hand, is the one who believes that some day, perhaps even tomorrow, he will have another ball, another world, another sphere, another life. And so he can begin to play with this earth, enjoy its monotony, and even be resigned to its pinpricks, for he knows that very soon he is going to have the other ball, which is the other life that will never wear out nor become tiresome, because its life is the life of the eternal God, the beginning and the end of all that is.

When, therefore, seized and suffused through and through with the Christian ideal of making Christ shine out in your life; and when in the routine of Christian living, you have begun your morning with a prayer and asked the Father's blessing on all your goings and comings; and when you have broken your fast with the Eucharistic Lord at the altar, and knelt in adoration before the uplifted Host and the glowing chalice; and when you have sanctified the day by offering each deed in union with the Master, and sanctified each trial by linking it with the Cross, and repressed unkind words and unjust criticisms out of love for Him Who prayed for His enemies on the Cross; and when the day is done you again kneel in thanksgiving and in humble gratitude to the Father of Light; and when after having done this day after day, week after week, and year after year in a constant effort to make your life more Christ-like; and then you wonder just what other thing needs to be done to bring you just a step closer to the goal of everlasting peace and happiness—then remember the lesson of the thrill of monotony, and "Do it again."

The way we live has an influence on the way we think. This is not a denial of the intellectual factors in belief, but merely an attempt to emphasize a neglected element. Some people imagine that they can bring a person to divine love merely by answering a doubt he has expressed. They assume that men are irreligious only because they are ignorant; that if atheists read a few good books or listened to a few choice arguments in favor of divinity, they would immediately embrace the faith. Religion seems to them to be a thing to be *known*, rather than a personality to be *embraced* and lived and loved. But Our Divine Lord, Who is truth itself, could not convince the Pharisees and certain sinners; they were intellectually confounded by His knowledge so that, after one encounter, no man dared question Him again—but still they did not believe. Christ told those who watched the resurrection of Lazarus that some of them would not believe, though one rose *daily* from the dead. Intellectual knowledge is not the "one thing necessary": not all the Ph.D.s are saints, and the ignorant are not demons. Indeed, a certain type of education may simply turn a man from a stupid egotist into a clever egotist, and of the two the former has the better chance of salvation.

It is easy to find truth; it is hard to face it, and harder still to follow it. Modern education is geared to what it calls "extending the frontiers of truth", and sometimes this ideal is prized and used to excuse men from acting on old truths already discovered. The discovery of the size of a distant star creates no moral obligation; but the old truths about the nature and destiny of man can be a reproach to the way one lives. Some psychologists and sociologists like to rap their knuckles at the door of truth about mankind, but they would run away if the door ever opened, showing man's contingency on God. The only people who ever arrive at a knowledge of God are those who, when the door is opened, accept that Truth and shoulder the responsibilities it brings. It requires more courage than brains to learn to know God: God is the most obvious fact of human experience, but accepting Him is one of the most arduous.

There are two nonintellectual factors which influence belief:

1. Good will.
2. Habits of living.

Why is it, when a strong intellectual argument for the faith is given to person *A* and person *B*, that *A* will accept and *B* will not? Since the cause is the same, the effect ought to be the same—but it is not. There must be some other factor present which makes one man embrace, the other reject, the truth—something in the mind it touches. A light striking a wall appears different from a light striking a window. Similarly this *x* factor, which makes for the rejection of divine truth in one case and its embrace in the other, is the will. As St. Thomas put it in his finely chiseled way: "Divine things are known in different ways by men according to the diversity of their attitudes. Those who have good will perceive Divine things according to Truth; those who have not good will perceive them in a confused way which makes them doubt and feel that they are mistaken."

What a man will intellectually accept depends to a great extent on what a man *is* or what he wants to be. The will, instead of admitting a truth presented to the mind, can ward it off and bar it out. God's pursuit of a mind is bound to fail unless the mind is also in pursuit of goodness. The message of the angels on Christmas night told us that only men with good will would become God's friends. This good-will factor is so important that it seems probable there is no such thing as intellectual atheism. Reason is on God's side, not the devil's; and to deny His absolute is to affirm a competing absolute. But if there is no intellectual atheism, there is a frequent atheism of the will, a deliberate rejection of God. That is why the psalmist places atheism not in the mind but in the heart: "The fool has said in his *heart*, there is no God." This primary requirement of good will holds not only for those who are looking for divine truth but also for those who have found it and who still make little progress spiritually. God's grace is never wanting to those who long to cooperate with it. The will to be wealthy makes men rich; the will to be Christ's makes men Christians.

Another factor affecting assent to the truth is our habit patterns. These patterns are the *result* of our failure to act upon the moral truths we already recognize. When the Christian truth comes to any mind, it is known according to the manner of the knower; and some knowers have a vast army of acts and habit patterns, prejudices and desires ready to war upon the divine purpose of life. What the mind receives is received against a background, which already forms a pattern of its own—and one it will reluctantly disarrange or change. In the face of divine truth, the habit patterns with their inferior motives arise to contest the high motive driving the mind toward the true. Then one may say: "I fear to believe because I will be ridiculed", or "because my family will not like it", or "because I will have to break with my companions and will make enemies".

Escapists who want a religion without a cross call themselves agnostics in order to avoid the moral consequences of truth. Agnosticism, scepticism, and cultivated doubt do not represent an intellectual position—for wherever there is a shadow there must be light, and negation would not exist if there were nothing to deny. These attitudes are rather a moral position, in which a person attempts to make himself invulnerable to divine truth by denying its existence and turning his back on it, as Pilate did. It is not doubts that cause our loose behavior, as often as such behavior causes doubts. Our Lord was extremely emphatic on this point: "Anyone who acts shamefully hates the light, will not come into the light, for fear that his doings will be found out. Whereas the man whose life is true comes to the light, so that his deeds may be seen for what they are, deeds done in God" (Jn 3:20–21). "You pore over the Scriptures, thinking to find eternal life in them (and indeed, it is of these I speak as bearing witness to me): but you will not come to me, to find life. I do not mean that I look for honour from men, but that I can see you have no love of God in your hearts" (Jn 5:39–42). St. Paul reaffirms his Savior: "They profess recognition of God, but their practice contradicts it; it is they who are abominable, who are disloyal, who are ill qualified for the practice of any true virtue" (Tit 1:16).

What is important is not *what* people say against God, or His Divine Son, Our Beloved Savior, or His Mystical Body, but *why* they say it. The "what" is often a rationalization of their habits of life. A fallen-away Catholic who says, "I can no longer believe in the Sacrament of Penance", really means, "I am leading an evil life, and I refuse

to break my habits of sin to make my peace with God."
Reason is used to create sham doubts and to weave cloaks
with which to cover our real motives. No wonder God
must judge us—we are so slow to judge ourselves.

There are three kinds of dirt that can accumulate as
habits on the window of the soul to keep God's grace
from coming in. These are carnal dirt, or inordinate love
of fleshly pleasures; money dirt, or the lust of possessions;
and egocentric dirt, or selfishness and vanity. Cleaning the
window of the soul even a little brings God much closer.
"Blessed are the clean of heart for they shall see God."

All human appeals, arguments, and coaxings toward
moral betterment—like all psychological appeals to a morally disordered soul—*are external to the person to be reformed.*
Since the action comes from without, the reformer can
only ring the bell—he cannot get inside of the house, and
he has no ally within its doors. An alcoholic may admit
that all the arguments a reformer or psychologist presents to him are true, but there is a world of difference
between knowing what is right and doing what is right.
It is conceivable that the alcoholic, knowing that he is
doing wrong, knows also that his will power, unaided,
is not capable of freeing him from his vice. Or he may
resent the effort of any other man to interfere with him:
precisely because of their extrinsic character, many legal
and humanistic reforms are regarded as an impertinence by
those they seek to help.

Divine action on the soul, on the other hand, is internal and is so incommunicably personal that the man may
sometimes feel that it is his own creation. The impact of
God on the soul is not that of a proselytist, for a proselytist
works from without, like one billiard ball upon another.
But God, although working through His Apostles, allows
their words to affect the soul from within by "immanent

activity", which is the characteristic method by which living things grow. When this actual grace of God gets into
the soul, it acts something like light, shining through a
Gothic window to suffuse it with a brilliance which the
stained glass does not have of and by itself. It is not easy to
describe this divine action on the soul, for it is as invisible
and as spiritual as a natural truth in the mind, although it is
not merely natural. The truth that two and two make four
takes up no space, no latitude or longitude in our minds—
yet it is there, and it can influence our thinking and our
actions. On the higher level, God acts in the intellect as
truth, and in the will as love. He sometimes strikes the soul
with a terrific mystical impact which demands a complete
break with everything external.

The soul itself may not be certain when the Divine
invasion has occurred. One might almost say that God
enters the soul like a thief in the night—we may choose
whether to welcome Him or to reject Him, but we cannot *prevent* Him from invading the soul that He has made.
As the sun rises without asking permission of the night,
so Divine Life invades us without consulting the darkness of our minds. God establishes His beachhead in our
most unsuspecting moments, almost in secret, without
our being consciously aware of Him. He comes as a sudden thought that springs into the mind, an intense desire
that moves the will. His entrance is imperceptible; in the
beginning, we do not know that it is He. We do not resist
Him, for we have no sense of an alien interference. We
may even think that the sudden upsurge of our spirit is
our own, with no suspicion that it comes from God—just
as we may think that our eyes do all the seeing, without
being conscious of their reliance on the sun. It is only later
that we understand, looking back, that the initiative was
divine and eternal.

The occasion on which the divine thief chooses to steal away our unhappiness may be a moment of satiety with sin, as it was with Léon Bloy, or the sight of death, as it was with St. Francis, or the closeness of the stars and the desert, as it was with Ernest Psichari, or the reading of a book, as it was with Jacques Maritain, or the sound of church bells, as it was with Paul Claudel. Whatever the external circumstances, they are of no importance; they are the occasions on which one individual has met God—but God can be met anywhere. Though God has reserved to Himself the right and power of acting in the soul, of soliciting it to virtue and distracting it from evil, nevertheless He has left man a choice between welcoming the God he finds in his soul or ordering Him out. But enter it He does, stirring the soul, agitating it, shaking the grates of the heart to get rid of the clinkers and ashes of sin, so that the faint sparks of grace may blaze and burn. One can dispute the plea for goodness if it is spoken by a voice outside ourselves—but this voice speaks within us, and it does not argue. Our choice is not between agreeing or disagreeing with God's revelation in our souls; the only alternatives are to embrace or to reject the appeal, whose verity we have to recognize.

Almost everyone today wants religion, but everyone wants a religion that does not cost too much; that is why Christianity has been watered down to suit the modern mind. Everyone wants good health, but not everyone believes in dieting or giving up things which are bad for the organism. In like manner, many have a vague aspiration for goodness without the will to implement it with sacrifice. The tens of thousands who in the past year tried to give up smoking cigarettes, and then, after twenty-four hours, saw their resolution go up in smoke, can testify how little the modern mind is prepared for any kind of real sacrifice or self-denial.

It is not easy to say "No" to oneself. That is why so many philosophers have erected a philosophy of life based on saying "Yes" to every impulse and desire while dignifying it with the name "self-expression". But the fact still remains that serious progress in every walk of life demands some form of restraint: the doctor, the lawyer, the athlete, the artist, the singer, the businessman must all learn to "scorn delights and live laborious days" if they are to attain their ideals. The expert in Oriental languages or archaeology cannot at the same time be a champion tennis player. In all walks of life, something must be sacrificed if something is to be gained; the mind is developed at the expense of the body, and the body at the expense of the mind.

Religion, too, requires sacrifice; it is not a crutch, but a cross. It is not an escape, it is a burden; not a flight, but a response. One leans on a crutch, but a cross rests on us. A coward can use a crutch, but it takes a hero to embrace a cross.

Let him who thinks the cross is easy admit that he is wrong, or that he has broken a relationship of love, and then strive to right the wrong by penance and self-discipline, and he will discover the courage it takes.

The cross is laid on the shoulders of our pride and envy, our lusts and our angers, until by its friction it wears them away, and thus brings us to the great abiding joys of life. Like a canary's, the best songs are learned in darkness. A canary will learn only snatches of song while there is light in the cage, but in darkness it learns the song until its heart is so full of it that it never forgets.

The springs of fresh water well up amid the brine of the salt sea, the fairest alpine flowers bloom in the most rugged mountain passes, and the noblest songs are the outcome of the profoundest agony of soul. No one would say that the gold leans on the crutch of fire when it is purified of its dross; nor that the marble leans on the crutch of the chisel as the hidden form is revealed. Alcoholism is the crutch of a man who cannot live with his own conscience; religion is the cross of a man who purifies his conscience and no longer needs the drug.

When the mother asked Our Lord that her two sons be placed at the right and left side of Him in His glory, she actually asked for two crutches. But Our Lord asked in return if they could drink of the chalice of self-forgetfulness and moral heroism. As snow is cold and yet warms and refreshes the earth, so afflictions and efforts at moral regeneration warm and perfect the soul. The crutch-leaners rot in honey; the cross-bearers are preserved in brine. After a forest fire has raged furiously, it is discovered that the seed of some of the pine cones have been released by the heat; so too, taking up the cross has been the condition of making souls first happy and then saints.

The escapists who call religion a crutch are like the blind who call those who see visionaries. A boat is not a crutch to a man who wishes to cross the river, nor is a pencil a crutch to a hand that wants to write. But the man who has not brains enough to write, or has not courage enough to learn will call the pencil a crutch. The heroes must be prepared for the mockery of the weak. Once the divine hero was flung on His Cross, the crutch-callers asked Him to come down. They knew that that kind of love was the death of self-love. Ever since, the world has been divided between those who call religion a crutch because, being lame, they think everyone else is lame, and those who call religion a cross and believe—"Take up your cross daily and follow Me."

Every quest for pleasure is fundamentally a striving for the infinite. Every pleasure attracts us because we hope, by savoring it, to get a foretaste of something that will exceed it in intensity and joy. One bird, one star, one book should be enough to fill the hunger of a man, but it is not: we find no satisfaction in anything, because our appetites are formed for everything. Like a great vessel that is launched, man moves insecurely in shallow waters, being made to skim the sea. To ask man to stop short of anything save the infinite is to nullify his nature; our greed for good is greater than the earth can gratify. All love of poetry is a cry, a moan, and a weeping; the more sublime and true it is, the deeper is its lament. If the joy of attaining something for which we longed ravishes the mind for an hour, it reverts, by evening, to the immensity of its still-unfulfilled desires.

Our hunger for the infinite is never quieted; even those disillusioned by excess of pleasures have always kept in their imagination a hope of somewhere finding a truer source of satisfaction than any they have tried. Our search for the never-ending love is never ended—no one could really love anything unless he thought of it as eternal. Not everyone gives a name to this infinity toward which he tends and for which he yearns, but it is what the rest of us call God.

The pursuit of pleasure is thus a token of man's higher nature, a symptom of his loneliness in this world. Torn between what he has, which surfeits him, and the far-off transcendent, which attracts him, every worldly man stands in grave danger of self-hatred and despair until he finds his true infinite in God. As Pascal put it: "The knowledge of God without a perception of man's misery causes pride, and the knowledge of man's misery without a perception of God causes despair. Knowledge of Jesus Christ constitutes the middle course, because in Him we find both God and our own misery."

You cannot keep God out; He has His own way of getting into the soul. There are two breaches in our walls;

two cracks in our armor; two hidden entrances to the soul through which God can enter. These are so much a part of our nature that we cannot alter them: when God made us he built them, like trap doors, in our natures. Even when our intellects bar God's passage by the false obstructions to belief that unsound thinking has erected, He is able to penetrate to us through the secret doors we have not known how to bolt.

The first of these trap doors in the soul is the love of goodness. As we chase after every isolated tidbit that attracts us by its good, the soul is really in pursuit of the whole and infinite goodness of God. Every quest of pleasure, every love of a friend, every approval of a good child, every comparison of good and better, implies some goodness beyond all these good things, for none of them completely fills our hearts. Every lesser good we approve intimates our longing for utter goodness, for God. To say that we want good things but not goodness, which is God-ness, is like saying that we love the sunbeams but we hate the sun, or we like the moonlight but despise the moon. The substance of the sun does not reach our room with the sunbeam, but some participation of it does; and, in like manner, no part of God is in the good apple, the good friend, but a participation of that goodness is always there. No one can love the good without implicitly loving goodness, and to that extent God creeps into the soul in its every wish and every joy.

Because of this human predilection for what is good, no life is made up entirely of actions that are intrinsically wicked. The murderer savors the true goodness of a good dinner; a thief responds to the virtue of a child; a gangster feeds soup to poor people out of honest generosity. Good deeds are mingled with evil deeds. No one is forever persecuting, sinning, blaspheming; sometimes a hardened sinner is engaged in planting a rose, nursing a sick friend, fixing a neighbor's tire. There are considerable hidden reserves of natural goodness in everyone; they live on stubbornly in company with his predominant passion, even if that is turned toward evil. Because there is something in us that escapes infection, we are never intrinsically wicked, never incurable, never "impossible". Those who see our good deeds admire us; and those who see only our bad deeds hold us low: that is why there can be such divergent judgment about a man. Even when the will is perverse—even when a creature is enthralled and captivated by one great sinful adhesion, which makes his days a flight from God toward lust or power—even then there are some few good and commendable acts which contradict his general attitude. These isolated acts of virtue are like a clean handle on a dirty bucket; with them, God can lift a soul to His Peace.

The second trap door by which God enters a soul in flight from Him is by its ennui, its boredom, its satiety, its fed-up-ness, its loneliness, its melancholy, its despair. No matter how many evils we may have chosen, we have never exhausted the possibilities of choice—the human is still free—his power of choice is never exhausted. Every libido, every passion, every craving of the body is finite, carnal, and its cravings, when satisfied, fail to content us. But in the life of the weary sensualist, there is still one choice that has never been made, one great chord that has not yet been struck. He has not tried the infinite. Statements like "I have seen life" and "I have tried everything" are never true, because the men who speak this way have not explored the greatest adventure of all. The rich man still asks: "What lack I yet to make me happy?" He knew, as all sensation seekers know, that gratifying every whim still leaves the deepest appetites unsatisfied. There is always still something to be had—something we need badly. We know, but we do not know everything; we love, but not forever. We eat, and we still hunger; we drink, and we still thirst: "The eye is not filled with seeing, neither is the ear filled with hearing" (Eccles 1:8).

Despite our efforts to find contentment in the temporal, we fail. For as the fish needs the water and the eye needs light, as the bird needs air and the grass needs earth, so the spiritual soul needs an Infinite God. Because God, for Whom we were made, is left out of its reckoning, the soul feels an emptiness, a boredom with what it has, a yearning for what it has not. This ennui is the negative presence of God in the soul—just as sickness is the negative presence of health in the body, and hunger is the negative presence of food in the stomach; a lack in us points to the existence of something capable of filling it. Through this trap door of our emptiness, God enters. If we do not admit Him at first, He will intensify the dissatisfaction and the loneliness, until finally He is accepted as our soul's guest and its eternal host.

2

Christ Helps Our Minds and Wills

The life of modern man is one of constant conflict. The
cause of conflict is not environment, because the golden
bit does not make the better horse; Judas, who had the
best environment in history, died in ignominy and shame.
Conflict is not due to ignorance; otherwise every D.D.
would be a saint. The conflict *is not due to the person alone.*
Personal sins do intensify one's complexes; but the inescapable fact is that every human person in the world has
a conflict going on inside him. Since it is not you, or I,
or he, or she alone that has a tension, it must be that the
conflict has not a personal origin but is due to *human nature*
itself. The source of the disorder is to be found both in
the individual and in humanity itself. A psychology which
assumed that all conflicts are due to aberrations in the person himself would fail to account for the universality of
conflict. Since everybody is that way, no individual or personal explanation can be the total cause. The personal
cause is an effect of the natural cause, as the individual sins
because human nature sinned.

If the true origin of the conflict is to be found, not in
the individual exclusively, but in human nature, it is well
to examine the human nature that is common to all of us.
Two facts stand out.

First, man is not an angel, nor is he a devil. He is not
intrinsically corrupt (as theologians began claiming four

hundred years ago) nor is he intrinsically divine (as philosophers began saying fifty years ago).[1] Rather, man has
aspirations to good which he finds it impossible to realize
completely by himself; at the same time, he has an incli-
nation toward evil which solicits him away from these
ideals. He is like a man who is down a well through his
own stupidity. He knows he ought not to be there, but he
cannot get out by himself. Or, to change the picture, he is
like a clock whose mainspring is broken. He needs to be
fixed on the inside, but the repairs must be supplied from
without. He is mistaken if he is an optimist, who believes
evolution will give him a mainspring, or a pessimist, who
believes that nobody can fix him. He is a creature who can
run well again, but only if some watchmaker will have the
kindness to repair him.

Second, this conflict has all the appearances of being due
to an abuse of human freedom. As the drunkard is what
he is because of an act of choice, so human nature seems
to have lost the original goodness with which a good God
endowed it through an act of choice. As St. Augustine
said, "Whatever we are, we are not what we ought to be."
The origin of this conflict has been told by medieval and
modern theologians through the analogy of music. Picture an orchestra on a stage with a celebrated conductor
directing the beautiful symphony he himself composed.
Each member of the orchestra is free to follow the conductor and thus to produce harmony. But each member
is also free to disobey the conductor. Suppose one of the
musicians deliberately plays a false note and then induces
a violinist alongside of him to do the same. Having heard
the discord, the conductor could do one of two things.
He could either strike his baton and order the measure

[1] Sheen is writing this in 1949—ED.

replayed, or he could ignore the discord. It would make no difference which he did, for that discord has already gone out into space at a certain temperature at the rate of about 1100 feet per second. On and on it goes, affecting even the infinitesimally small radiations of the universe. As a stone dropped in a pond causes a ripple which affects the most distant shore, so this discord affects even the stars. As long as time endures, somewhere in God's universe there is a disharmony, introduced by the free will of man.

Could that discord be stopped? Not by man himself, for man could never reach it; time is irreversible, and man is localized in space. It *could*, however, be stopped by the Eternal coming out of His agelessness into time, laying hold of that false note, arresting it in its flight. But would it still be a discord even in God's hands? No! Not if God wrote a *new* symphony and made that false note its first note! Then all would be harmony again.

A long time ago, long before Oedipus and Electra, God wrote a beautiful symphony of creation; chemicals, flowers, and animals were subject to man, man's passions were under the guidance of reason, and man's personality was in love with Love, which is God. God gave that symphony to man and woman to play, with a complete set of directions, down to the last detail of what to avoid. Man and woman, being free, could obey the divine director and produce harmony, or they could disobey Him. The devil suggested that, because the divine director had marked the script and told them what to play and what not to play, He was destroying their freedom. The woman first succumbed to the idea that freedom is license, or absence of law; she struck a discord to prove her so-called "independence". It was a very unladylike thing to do. She then induced man to do the same—which was a very ungentlemanly thing to do. On and on through the whole human race this original discord swept; whenever there was the conjunction of man and woman, it affected every human being, who ever was born, save one, for each inherited the effects of that disharmony. The discord even had its repercussions in the material universe, as thistles grew and beasts became wild. As a stream polluted at its source passes on the pollution through its length, so the original fault was transmitted to mankind.

That original discord could not be stopped by man himself, because he could not repair an offense against the infinite with his finite self. He had contracted a bigger debt than he could pay. The debt could be paid only by the divine master musician coming out of His eternity into time. But there is a world of difference between stopping a discordant note and a rebellious man. One has no freedom, the other has; and God refuses to be a totalitarian dictator in order to abolish evil by destroying human freedom. God could seize a note, but He would not seize a man. Instead of conscripting man, God willed to consult mankind again as to whether or not it wanted to be made a member of the divine orchestra once more.

Out from the great white throne of light, there comes an angel of light, down past the plains of Esdralon to the little village of Nazareth to a village maid called Mary. Since a woman struck the first discordant note, a woman would be given the chance to right it. This woman herself was free from the stain of the original sin through the anticipated merits of the Son she was later to bear. Fitting it was that He Who is innocence itself should come through portals of flesh not polluted with its common sin. This privilege of Mary has been called the Immaculate Conception. Since a fallen angel tempted the first woman to rebel, God now consults through an unfallen angel, Gabriel, with the new Eve, Mary, and asks, "Will you give me a man? Will you give me freely a new note out of mankind with which I can write a new symphony?" This new man must *be* a man; otherwise God would not be acting in the name of mankind. But he must also be outside the current of infection to which all men are subject. Being born of a woman, He will be a man; being born of a Virgin, He will be a sinless man. The Virgin was asked if she would consent to be a Mother. Since there could be no birth without love, in the case of the Blessed Virgin Mary, the fire and passion of the Spirit of Love overshadowed her, and He that was born of her is the Son of God, the Son of Man, and His name is Jesus, because He saved the world from its sins.

The Immaculate Conception and the Virgin Birth were to the beginning of a new mankind something like what a lock is to a canal, the former in a special way. If a ship is sailing on a polluted canal and wishes to transfer itself to clear waters on a higher level, it must pass through a device which locks out the polluted waters and raises the ship to the higher position. Then the other gate of the lock is lifted, and the ship rides on the new, clear waters, taking none of the polluted waters with it. Mary's Immaculate Conception was like that lock, inasmuch as, through her, mankind passed from the lower level of the sons of Adam to the higher level of the sons of God.

When this plan was presented to Mary in the greatest charter of freedom the world ever heard, she answered, "Be it done unto me according to Thy Word." And God began taking on the form of man within her chaste body. Nine months later the Eternal established its beachhead in Bethlehem, as He Who is eternal appeared in time; the bird that built the nest is hatched therein; He Who made the world is born in the world which received Him not. Because He is man, Jesus Christ can act in the name of man and be responsible as man; because He is God, everything He does with that human nature has an infinite value. Through this human nature of His which is sinless, He makes Himself responsible for all the sins of the world, and to such an extent that in the strong language of St. Paul, "He is made sin." As a rich brother takes on himself the debt of his bankrupt brother, so Our Lord takes upon Himself all the discords, disharmonies, all the sins, guilts, and blasphemies of man, as if He Himself were guilty. As gold is thrust into the furnace to have its dross burned away, so He takes His human nature and plunges it into the fires of Calvary to have our sins burned away. To change the figure again—since sin is in the blood, He pours out His blood in redemption; for without the shedding of blood there is no remission of sins.

History is full of men who have claimed that they came from God, or that they were gods, or that they bore messages from God—Buddha, Mohammed, Confucius, Christ, Lao-tze, and thousands of others, right down to the person who founded a new religion this very day. Each of them has a right to be heard and considered. But as a yardstick external to and outside of whatever is to be measured is needed, so there must be some permanent tests available to all men, all civilizations, and all ages, by which they can decide whether any one of these claimants, or all of them, are justified in their claims. These tests are of two kinds: *reason* and *history*. Reason, because everyone has it, even those without faith; history, because everyone lives in it and should know something about it.

Reason dictates that if any one of these men actually came from God, the least thing that God could do to support His claim would be to pre-announce His coming. Automobile manufacturers tell their customers when to expect a new model. If God sent anyone from Himself, or if He came Himself with a vitally important message for all men, it would seem reasonable that He would first let men know when His messenger was coming, where He would be born, where He would live, the doctrine He would teach, the enemies He would make, the program He would adopt for the future, and the manner of His death. By the extent to which the messenger conformed with these announcements, one could judge the validity of his claims.

Reason further assures us that if God did not do this, then there would be nothing to prevent any impostor from appearing in history and saying, "I come from God", or "An angel appeared to me in the desert and gave me this message." In such cases there would be no objective, historical way of testing the messenger. We would have only his word for it, and of course he could be wrong.

If a visitor came from a foreign country to Washington and said he was a diplomat, the government would ask him for his passport and other documents testifying that he represented a certain government. His papers would have to antedate his coming. If such proofs of identity are asked from delegates of other countries, reason certainly ought to do so with messengers who claim to have come from God. To each claimant reason says, "What record was there before you were born that you were coming?"

With this test one can evaluate the claimants. (And at this preliminary stage, Christ is no greater than the others.) Socrates had no one to foretell his birth. Buddha had no one to pre-announce him and his message or tell the day when he would sit under the tree. Confucius did not have the name of his mother and his birthplace recorded, nor were they given to men centuries before he arrived so that when he did come, men would know he was a messenger from God. But, with Christ it was different. Because of the Old Testament prophecies, His coming was not unexpected. There were no predictions about Buddha,

Confucius, Lao-tze, Mohammed, or anyone else; but there were predictions about Christ. Others just came and said, "Here I am, believe me." They were, therefore, only men among men and not the Divine in the human. Christ alone stepped out of that line saying, "Search the writings of the Jewish people and the related history of the Babylonians, Persians, Greeks, and Romans." (For the moment, pagan writings and even the Old Testament may be regarded only as historical documents, not as inspired works.)

It is true that the prophecies of the Old Testament can be best understood in the light of their fulfillment. The language of prophecy does not have the exactness of mathematics. Yet if one searches out the various Messianic currents in the Old Testament, and compares the resulting picture with the life and work of Christ, can one doubt that the ancient predictions point to Jesus and the kingdom which He established? God's promise to the patriarchs that through them all the nations of the earth would be blessed; the prediction that the tribe of Judah would be supreme among the other Hebrew tribes until the coming of Him Whom all nations would obey; the strange yet undeniable fact that in the Bible of the Alexandrian Jews, the Septuagint, one finds clearly predicted the *Virgin* Birth of the Messiah; the prophecy of Isaiah 53 about the patient sufferer, the servant of the Lord, who will lay down his life as a guilt-offering for his people's offenses; the perspectives of the glorious, everlasting kingdom of the House of David—in whom but Christ have these prophecies found their fulfillment? From a historical point of view alone, here is uniqueness which sets Christ apart from all other founders of world religions. And once the fulfillment of these prophecies did historically take place in the person of Christ, not only did all prophecies cease in Israel, but there was discontinuance of sacrifices when the true Paschal Lamb was sacrificed.

A second distinguishing fact is that once He appeared, He struck history with such impact that He split it in two, dividing it into two periods: one before His coming, the other after it. Buddha did not do this, nor any of the great Indian philosophers. Even those who deny God must date their attacks upon Him, A.D. so and so, or so many years after His coming.

Every other person who ever came into this world came into it to live—He came into it to die. Death was a stumbling block to Socrates—it interrupted his teaching. But to Christ, death was the goal and fulfillment of His life, the gold that He was seeking. Few of His words or actions are intelligible without reference to His Cross. He presented Himself as a savior rather than merely as a teacher. It meant nothing to teach men to be good unless He also gave them the power to be good, after rescuing them from the frustration of guilt.

The story of every human life begins with birth and ends with death. In the person of Christ, however, *it was His death that was first and His life that was last.* Scripture describes Him as "the Lamb slain as it were, from the beginning of the world". He was slain in intention by the first sin and rebellion against God. It was not so much that His birth cast a shadow on His life and thus led to His death; it was rather that the Cross was first, and cast its shadow back to His birth. His has been the only life in the world that was ever lived backward. As the flower in the crannied wall tells the poet of nature, and as the atom is the miniature of the solar system, so too His birth tells the mystery of the gibbet. He went from the known to the known, from the reason of His coming manifested by His name "Jesus" or "Savior" to the fulfillment of His coming, namely, His death on the Cross.

John gives us His eternal prehistory; Matthew, His temporal prehistory, by way of His genealogy. It is significant how much His temporal ancestry was connected with sinners and foreigners! These blots on the escutcheon of His human lineage suggest a pity for the sinful and for the strangers to the Covenant. Both these aspects of His compassion would later on be hurled against Him as accusations: "He is a friend of sinners"; "He is a Samaritan." But the shadow of a stained past foretells His future love for the stained. Born of a woman, He was a man and could be one with all mankind; born of a Virgin, who was overshadowed by the Spirit and "full of grace", He would also be outside that current of sin which infected all men.

Where did this divine life come from? It came from heaven in the person of Jesus Christ, the Son of God, Who became man.

One night there went out over the stillness of the evening breeze, out over those white chalky hills of Bethlehem, a cry, a gentle cry, the cry of a new born babe. "The Word became flesh and dwelt amongst us." Earth did not hear the cry, for the earth slept; men did not hear the cry, for they did not know that a child could be greater than a man; the sea did not hear the cry, for the sea was filled with its own voice; kings did not hear the cry, for they did not know that a king could be born in a stable; empires did not hear the cry, for empires did not know that an infant could hold the reins that steer suns and worlds in their courses. But shepherds and philosophers heard the cry, for only the very simple and the very learned—never the man with one book—know that the heart of a god can cry out in the cry of a child. And they came with gifts—and adored, and so great was the majesty seated on the brow of the child which lay before them, so great was the dignity of the babe, so powerful was the light of those eyes that shone like celestial suns, that they could not help but cry out: "Emmanuel: God is with us." God revealed Himself to men again. This time He shone through the prism of the Incarnation and brought divine life to human life. He Who is born without a mother in heaven is born without a father on earth. He Who made His Mother is born of His Mother. He Who made all flesh is born of flesh. "The bird that built the nest is hatched therein." Maker of the sun, under the sun; Molder of the earth, on the earth; ineffably wise, a little infant. Filling the world, lying in a manger; ruling the stars, suckling a breast; the mirth of heaven weeps; God becomes man; Creator a creature. Rich become poor; divinity incarnate; majesty subjugated; liberty captive; eternity time; master a servant; truth accused; judge judged; justice condemned; Lord scourged; power bound with ropes; king crowned with thorns; salvation wounded; Life dead. "The eternal word is dumb." Marvel of marvels! Union of unions! Three mysterious unions in one: divinity and humanity; virginity and fecundity; faith and the heart of man. And though we shall live on through eternity, eternity will not be long enough for us to understand the mystery of that "Child who was a father and of the Mother who was a child."

For the first time in the history of the redeemed universe is the divine hypostatically bound up with human nature. That very life of God that passes from Father to Son in the eternal generation of the Trinity, now passes into the world and assumes a human nature like our own, graces it with the plenitude of His divinity, and gives us that message of hope: "I am come that you may have life and that in abundance"—not the physical life which dies, but the spiritual life which endureth unto life everlasting. Christ does not fit, as the other world teachers do, into the established category of a *good* man. Good men do not lie. But if Christ was not all that He said He was, namely, the Son of the living God, the Word of God in the flesh, then He was not "just a good man"; then He was a knave, a liar, a charlatan and the greatest deceiver who ever lived. If He was not what He said He was, the Christ, the Son of God, He was the anti-Christ! If He was only a man, then He was not even a "good" man.

But He was *not only* a man. He would have us either worship Him or despise Him—despise Him as a mere man, or worship Him as true God and true man. That is the alternative He presents.

When one takes into account also His reiterated assertions about His divinity—such as asking us to love Him above parents, to believe in Him even in the face of persecution, to be ready to sacrifice our bodies in order to save our souls in union with Him—to call Him just a good man ignores the facts. No man is good unless he is humble; and humility is a recognition of truth concerning oneself. A man who thinks he is greater than he actually is is not humble, but a vain and boastful fool. How can any man claim prerogatives over conscience, and over history, and over society and the world, and still claim he is "meek and humble of heart"? But if He is God as well as man, His language falls into place and everything that He says is intelligible. But if He is not what He claimed to be, then some of His most precious sayings are nothing but bombastic outbursts of self-adulation that breathe rather the spirit of Lucifer than the spirit of a good man. What avails Him to proclaim the law of self-renouncement, if He Himself renounces truth to call Himself God? Even His sacrifice on the Cross becomes a suspect and a dated thing, when it goes hand in hand with delusions of grandeur and infernal conceit. He could not be called even a sincere teacher, for no sincere teacher would allow anyone to construe his claims to share the rank and the name of the great God in heaven.

The choice that lies before men is either the hypothesis of culpable insincerity or the fact that He spoke the literal truth and, therefore, must be taken at His word. It is easier to believe that God has achieved His works of wonder and mercy in His Divine Son on earth than to close the moral eye to the brightest spot that meets it in human history, and thus lapse into despair. No human could be good, aye! he would be arrogant and blasphemous, to have made the assertions He did concerning Himself. Instead of being above His moral followers who call themselves Christians, He would have been infinitely below the level of the worst of them. It is easier to believe what He said about Himself, namely, that He is God, than to explain how the world could ever have taken as a model such an unmitigated liar, such a contemptuous boaster. It is only because Jesus is God that the human character of Jesus is a manifestation of the divine.

We must either lament His madness or adore His person, but we cannot rest on the assumption that He was a professor of ethical culture. Rather, one can say with Chesterton, "Expect the grass to wither and the birds to drop dead out of the air, when a strolling carpenter's apprentice says calmly and almost carelessly, like one looking over his shoulder: 'Before Abraham was, I am.'" The Roman sergeant, who had his own gods and was hardened both to war and death, came to the answer during the Crucifixion when both his reason and his conscience affirmed the truth:

Truly, this is the Son of God.

What men call the Incarnation is but the union of two natures, the divine and the human, in a single person who governs both. This is not difficult to understand; for what is man but a sample, at an immeasurably lower level, of a union of two totally different substances, one material and the other immaterial, one the body, the other the soul, under the regency of a single human personality? What are more remote from one another than powers and capacities of flesh and spirit? Antecedent to their unity, how difficult it would be ever to conceive of a moment when body and soul would be united in a single personality. That they are so united is an experience clear to every mortal. And yet it is an experience at which man does not marvel because of its familiarity.

God, Who brings together body and soul into one human personality, notwithstanding their difference of nature, could surely bring about the union of a human body and a human soul with His divinity under the control of His eternal person. This is what is meant by "And the Word was made flesh, and came to dwell among us" (Jn 1:14).

The Person Who assumed human nature was not created, as is the case of all other persons. His Person was the pre-existent Word or *Logos*. His human nature, on the other hand, was derived from the Miraculous Conception by Mary, in which the divine overshadowing of the Spirit and the human *Fiat*, or the consent of a woman, were most beautifully blended. This is the beginning of a new humanity out of the material of the fallen race. When the Word became flesh, it did not mean that any change took place in the divine Word. The Word of God proceeding forth did not leave the Father's side. What happened was not so much the conversion of the Godhead into flesh, as the taking of a manhood into God.

There was continuity with the fallen race of man through the manhood taken from Mary; there is discontinuity through the fact that the person of Christ is the pre-existent *Logos*. Christ thus literally becomes the second Adam, the man through Whom the human race starts all over. His teaching centered on the incorporation of human natures to Him, after the manner in which the human nature that He took from Mary was united to the eternal Word.

It is hard for a man to understand the humility that was involved in the Word becoming flesh. Imagine, if it were possible, a human person divesting himself of his body, and then sending his soul into the body of a serpent. A double humiliation would follow: first, accepting the limitations of a serpentine organism, knowing all the while his mind was superior, and that fangs could not adequately articulate thoughts no serpent ever possessed. The second humiliation would be to be forced as a result of this "emptying of self" to live in the companionship of serpents. But all this is nothing compared to the emptying of God, by which He took on the form of man and accepted the limitations of humanity, such as hunger and persecution; not trivial either was it for the wisdom of God to condemn itself to association with poor fishermen who knew so little. But this humiliation which began in Nazareth when He was conceived in the Virgin Mary was only the first of many to counteract the pride of man, until the final humiliation of death on the Cross. If there had been no Cross, there would have been no crib; if there had been no nails, there would have been no straw. But He could not teach the lesson of the Cross as payment for sin; He had to *take* it. God the Father did not spare His Son—so much did He love mankind. That was the secret wrapped in the swaddling bands.

One way to make enemies and antagonize people is to challenge the spirit of the world. The world has a spirit, as each age has a spirit. There are certain unanalyzed assumptions which govern the conduct of the world. Anyone who challenges these worldly maxims, such as, "You only live once", "Get as much out of life as you can", "Who will ever know about it?" "What is sex for if not for pleasure?" is bound to make himself unpopular.

In the Beatitudes, Our Divine Lord takes those eight flimsy catchwords of the world—"security", "revenge", "laughter", "popularity", "getting even", "sex", "armed might", and "comfort"—and turns them upside down. To those who say, "You cannot be happy unless you are rich", He says, "Blessed are the poor in spirit." To those who say, "Don't let him get away with it", He says, "Blessed are the patient." To those who say, "Laugh and the world laughs with you", He says, "Blessed are those who mourn." To those who say, "If nature gave you sex instincts you ought to give them free expression, otherwise you will become frustrated", He says, "Blessed are the clean of heart." To those who say, "Seek to be popular and well known", He says, "Blessed are you when men revile you and persecute you and speak all manner of evil against you falsely because of Me." To those who say, "In time of peace prepare for war", He says, "Blessed are the peacemakers."

The cheap clichés around which movies are written and novels composed, He scorns. He proposes to burn what they worship; to conquer errant sex instincts instead of allowing them to make slaves of man; to tame economic conquests instead of making happiness consist in an abundance of things external to the soul. All false beatitudes which make happiness depend on self-expression, license, having a good time, or "Eat, drink, and be merry for tomorrow you die", He scorns because they bring mental disorders, unhappiness, false hopes, fears, and anxieties.

The key to the Sermon on the Mount is the way He used two expressions: one was, "You have heard"; the other was the short, emphatic word "But". When He said, "You have heard", He reached back to what human ears had heard for centuries and still hear from ethical reformers—all those rules and codes and precepts which are half measures between instinct and reason, between local customs and the highest ideals. When He said, "You have heard", He included the Mosaic Law, Buddha with his eightfold way, Confucius with his rules for being a gentleman, Aristotle with his natural happiness, the broadness of the Hindus, and all the humanitarian groups of our day, who would translate some of the old codes into their own language and call them a new way of life. Of all these compromises, He said, "You have heard."

"You have heard that it was said, 'Thou shalt not commit adultery.'" Moses had said it; pagan tribes suggested it; primitive peoples respected it. Then came the terrible and awful "But": "But I tell you. . . ." "But I tell you that he who casts his eye on a woman so as to lust after her, has already committed adultery with her in his own heart." Our Lord went into the soul, and laid hold of thought, and branded even the *desire* for sin as a sin. If it was wrong to do a certain thing, it was wrong to think about that thing. He would say, "Away with your hygiene which tries to keep hands clean after they have stolen, and bodies free from disease after they have ravished another." He went into the depths of the heart, and branded even the intention to sin a sin. He did not wait for the evil tree to bear evil fruits. He would prevent the very sowing of the evil seed. Wait not until your hidden sins come out as psychoses and neuroses and compulsions. Get rid of them at their sources. Repent! Purge! Evil that can be put into statistics, or that can be locked in jails, is too late to remedy.

Christ affirmed that when a man married a woman, he married both her body and her soul; he married the whole person. If he got tired of the body, he might not thrust her body away for another, since he was still responsible for her soul. So He thundered, "You have heard." In that expression He summarized the jargon of every decaying civilization. "You have heard, 'Get a divorce; God does not expect you to live without happiness'"; then came the "But". "But I tell you that the man who puts away his wife makes an adulteress of her, and whoever marries her after she has been put away, commits adultery" (Mt 5:32).

What matters if the body is lost? The soul is still there, and that is worth more than the thrill a body can give, more even than the universe itself. He would keep men and women pure, not from contagion, but from desire of another; to imagine a betrayal is in itself a betrayal. So He declared: "What God has joined, let not man put asunder" (Mk 10:9).

No man! No judge! No nation!

The Sermon on the Mount is so much at variance with all that our world holds dear that the world will crucify anyone who tries to live up to its values. Because Christ preached them, He had to die. Calvary was the price He paid for the Sermon on the Mount. Only mediocrity survives. Those who call black black and white white are sentenced for intolerance. Only the grays live.

The Beatitudes cannot be taken alone: they are not ideals; they are hard facts and realities inseparable from the Cross of Calvary. What He taught was self-crucifixion: to love those who hate us; to pluck out eyes and cut off arms in order to prevent sinning; to be clean on the inside when the passions clamor for satisfaction on the outside; to forgive those who would put us to death; to overcome evil with good; to bless those who curse us; to stop mouthing freedom until we have justice, truth, and love of God in our hearts as the condition of freedom; to live in the world and still keep oneself unpolluted from it; to deny ourselves sometimes legitimate pleasures in order the better to crucify our egotism—all this is to sentence the old man in us to death.

Those who heard Him preach the Beatitudes were invited to stretch themselves out on a cross, to find happiness on a higher level by death to a lower order, to despise all the world holds sacred, and to venerate as sacred all the world regards as an ideal. Heaven is happiness; but it is too much for man to have two heavens, an *ersatz* one below, and a real one above. Hence the four "woes" He immediately added to the Beatitudes. "Woe upon you who are rich, you have your comfort already. Woe upon you who are filled full; you shall be hungry. Woe upon you who laugh now; you shall mourn and weep. Woe upon you when all men speak well of you; their fathers treated the false prophets no worse" (Lk 6:24–26).

Crucifixion cannot be far away when a Teacher says "woe" to the rich, the satiated, the lighthearted, and the popular. Truth is not in the Sermon on the Mount alone; it is in the One Who lived out the Sermon on the Mount on Golgotha. The four woes would have been ethical condemnations, if He had not died full of the opposite of the four woes: poor, abandoned, sorrowful, and despised. On the Mount of the Beatitudes, He bade men hurl themselves on the cross of self-denial; on the Mount of Calvary, He embraced that very cross. Though the shadow of the Cross would not fall across the place of the skull until three years later, it was already in His Heart the day He preached on "How to Be Happy."

Just as sex is a God-given instinct for the prolongation of the human race, so the desire for property as a prolongation of one's ego is a natural right sanctioned by natural law. A person is free on the inside because he can call his soul his own; he is free on the outside because he can call property his own. Internal freedom is based upon the fact that "I am"; external freedom is based on the fact that "I have". But just as the excesses of flesh produce lust, for lust is sex in the wrong place, as dirt is matter in the wrong place, so there can be a deordination of the desire for property until it becomes greed, avarice, and capitalistic aggression.

In order to atone, repair, and make up for excess of avarice and selfishness, Our Blessed Lord gave a lesson in self-sacrifice. The occasion was an enquiring young man. Our Blessed Lord had a chance to win him as a follower; but when He spoke of the Cross, He lost him. The young man wanted the prize, but the cost was too great. The youth who came was rich and also a synagogue official. The desire to be associated with Our Lord was manifested by the fact that he came running to Him and fell at His feet. As regards the uprightness of the youth there could be no doubt; his question to Our Lord was: "Master, who art so good, what good must I do to win eternal life?" (Mt 19:16).

"Why dost thou call me good? None is good except God only" (Mk 10:18).

Our Lord was not objecting to being called good, but to being taken merely as a good teacher. The young man had addressed Him as a great teacher, but still as a man; he had admitted goodness, but still on the level of human goodness. If He were merely a man the title of essential goodness would not belong to Him. There was hidden in His answer an affirmation of His deity; God alone is good. He was, therefore, inviting the young man to cry out, "Thou art Christ, the Son of the living God."

When the young man asked: "Where is it that I am still wanting?" (Mt 19:20), Our Lord answered: "If thou hast a mind to be perfect, go home and sell all that belongs to thee; give it to the poor, and so the treasure thou hast shall be in heaven; then come back and follow me" (Mt 19:21). There was no condemnation of wealth here; but there was a higher perfection than the human. As a man might leave his wife, so also a man might leave his property. The Cross would demand that souls give up what they loved most and be content with the treasure in God's hands. One may ask, Why did the Lord ask for such a sacrifice? The Savior allowed Zacchaeus the tax collector to keep half his goods; Joseph of Arimathea, after the Crucifixion, was described as rich; the property of Ananias was his own; Our Lord ate in the home of His wealthy friends in Bethany. But here it was a question of a young man who asked what was still wanting in the way of perfection. When the Lord proposed to him the ordinary way of salvation, namely, keeping the Commandments, the youth was dissatisfied. He sought for something more perfect; but when the perfect way was proposed to him, namely, renunciation: "The young man went away sad at heart, for he had great possessions" (Mt 19:22). There are degrees in the love of God, one common and the other heroic. The common was the keeping of the Commandments; the heroic was renouncement, the taking-up of the cross of voluntary poverty. The earnestness of the youth vanished; he kept his possessions and he lost the One who would give him the Cross. Though the young man kept his possessions, he is described as going away "sorrowful".

When the young man left, Our Lord said to His Apostles: "With what difficulty will those who have riches enter God's kingdom! ... It is easier for a camel to pass through a needle's eye, than for a man to enter the kingdom of God when he is rich" (Mk 10:23–25).

Many individuals disclaim responsibilities for the faults and failings of a collectivity. For example, when there is corruption in government, individuals often deny that they are involved. The more sinless people are, the more greatly they disclaim all relationship to those that are sinners. They almost assume that their responsibility varies in direct ratio with their sinfulness. Their argument is that since they are not responsible for the mistakes of society, they are not involved.

Actually, the contrary is true in those who are *most* sinless. The greater the sinlessness, the greater the sense of the responsibility and awareness of corporate guilt. The truly good man feels the world is the way it is because in some way he has not been better. The keener the moral sensitiveness, the greater is the compassion for those languishing under a burden. This can become so deep that the other person's agony is directly felt as one's own. The only person in the world who had eyes to see would want to be a staff to the blind; the only person in the world who was healthy would want to minister to the sick.

What is true of physical suffering is also true of moral evil. Hence, the sinless Christ took on the ills of the world. As the more healthy are better able to minister to the sick, so too the more innocent can better atone for the guilt of others. A lover would, if possible, take on the sufferings of the beloved. Divinity took on the moral ills of the world as if they were His own. Being man, He shared in them; being God, He could redeem for them.

Calvary was no interruption of His life activities, no tragic and premature spoiling of His plan, no evil end which hostile forces would impose upon Him. The giving of His life was of the pattern of martyrs for righteousness, and of patriarchs for glorious causes. The purpose of His life, He said, was to pay a ransom for the liberation of the slaves of sin; this was a divine "must" that was laid upon Him when He came into the world. His death was offered in payment for evil. If men were only in error, He might have been a teacher fenced in by all the comforts of life; and after having taught the theory of pain, He would die on a soft bed. But then He would have left no other message than a code to obey. But if men were in sin, He would be a redeemer and His message would be "Follow Me", to share in the fruit of that redemption.

Not everyone, however, chooses to follow Christ, the Light of the world. This is not to say that men begin with a conscious hatred of the Light, because truth is as native to the mind as light to the eye. But when that Light shone on their souls and revealed their sins, they hated it just as the bank robber hates the searchlight the policeman has turned on him. The truth which He brought, men recognized as a claim on their allegiance, because they were made for it; but since they had perverted their natures by evil behavior, His truth stirred their consciences and they despised it. All their habits of life, their dishonesties and baser passions, roused them in violent opposition to that Light. Many a sick man will not undergo a medical examination, for fear the doctor may tell him something he does not like. He told them therefore that He was not a teacher asking for a disciple who would parrot His sayings; He was a savior who first disturbed a conscience and then purified it. But many would never get beyond hating the disturber. The Light is no boon, except to those who are men of good will; their lives may be evil, but at least they want to be good. His presence, He said, was a threat to sensuality, avarice, and lust. When a man has lived in a dark cave for years, his eyes cannot stand the light of the sun; so the man who refuses to repent turns against mercy. No one can prevent the sun from shining, but every man can pull down the blinds and shut it out.

Christ said that no one could be indifferent to Him. Every man, He claimed, had some contact with Him. He is free to reject His influence, but the rejection is the stone which crushes him. No one can remain indifferent once he has met Him. He remains the perpetual element in the character of every hearer. No teacher in the world ever claimed that rejecting him would harden one's heart and make a man worse. But here is One who, within three days of going to His death, said that the very rejection of Him would decay the heart. Whether one believes or disbelieves Him, one is never the same afterward. Christ said that He was either the rock on which men would build the foundation of life, or the rock which would crush them. Never did men just simply pass Him by; He is the abiding presence. Some may think that they allow Him to pass by without receiving Him, but this He called fatal neglect. A fatal crushing would follow not only neglect or indifference, but also when there was formal opposition. No teacher who ever lived told those who heard him that the rejection of his words would mean their damnation. Even those who believe that Christ was only a teacher would scruple at this judgment about receiving His message. But as He was primarily a savior, the alternative was understandable. To reject the savior was to reject salvation, as Our Lord called Himself in the house of Zacchaeus. The questioners of His authority had no doubt of the spiritual significance of the parable and the reference to themselves. Their motives were discovered, which only exasperated more those whose designs were evil. When evil is revealed in the light, it does not always repent; sometimes it becomes more evil.

The good repent on knowing their sin; the evil become angry when discovered. Ignorance is not the cause of evil, as Plato held; neither is education the answer to the removal of evil. These men had an intellect as well as a will; knowledge as well as intention. Truth can be known and hated; goodness can be known and crucified.

The Spirit of Christ in man convinces him of sin. Nothing but the spirit can convince man of sin; conscience could not, for it can sometimes be smothered; public opinion cannot, for it sometimes justifies sin; but the gravest sin of all which the Spirit would reveal would not be intemperance, avarice, or lust, but unbelief in Christ. It is this same Spirit of God which renders the sinner not merely conscious of his state, but also contrite and penitent, when he accepts redemption.

To reject the Redeemer is to prefer evil to good. The crucifix is an autobiography in which man can read the story of his own life, either to his own salvation or his own condemnation. So long as sin was regarded only from a psychological point of view, the Cross of Christ appeared as an exaggeration. The sand of the desert, the blood of a beast, or water could just as well purify man. But once sin was seen under the sight of infinite holiness, then the Cross of Christ alone could equal and satisfy for this tragic horror.

Once man is convinced of his own sinfulness, he cannot be convinced of his own righteousness; once a man is convinced that Christ has saved him from sin, then he is convinced that Christ is his righteousness.

To have accepted Christ as our righteousness and to have embraced His holy faith is no guarantee of freedom from trials. The Divine Savior never said to His Apostles: "Be good and you will not suffer"; but He did say: "In this world you shall have tribulation." He told them also not to fear those that kill the body, but rather to fear those who can kill the soul. Now He told the Apostles that His life was a model for all of His followers; they were encouraged to take the worst this life had to offer with courage and serenity. He said that all sufferings were as the shade of "His hand outstretched caressingly". No talisman was He to promise as security from trials; rather as a captain

He went into battle in order to inspire men to transfigure some of life's greatest pains into the richest gains of the spiritual life. As the poet Edward Shillito has put it: "No false gods, immune from pain and sorrow, could console us in these days."

JESUS OF THE SCARS

If we have never sought, we seek Thee now;
  Thine eyes burn through the dark, our only stars;
We must have sight of thorn-pricks on Thy brow,
  We must have Thee, O Jesus of the Scars.

The heavens frighten us; they are too calm;
  In all the universe we have no place.
Our wounds are hurting us; where is the balm?
  Lord Jesus, by Thy Scars we claim Thy grace.

If when the doors are shut, Thou drawest near,
  Only reveal those hands, that side of Thine;
We know to-day what wounds are, have no fear,
  Show us Thy Scars, we know the countersign.
The other gods were strong; but Thou wast weak;
  They rode, but Thou didst stumble to a throne;
But to our wounds only God's wounds can speak,
  And not a god has wounds, but Thou alone.[2]

Edward Shillito, 1872–1948

Christ's title "the Son of Man" meant that He was representative not of the Jews alone, nor of the Samaritans alone, but of all mankind. His relation to mankind was similar, as we have said, to that of Adam. He was made

[2] From the book entitled *Masterpieces of Religious Verse*, ed. James Dalton Morrison (New York: Harper & Brothers, 1948). Reprinted by permission.

man and qualified Himself for copartnership with human nature. He entered into the reality of common humanity. He assumed a human nature into His sacred person. Aristotle said that if the gods take interest in human affairs, they may be expected to look with most satisfaction on what is most akin to their own nature. This would imply a certain amount of disdain for the human; hence the Greeks said that manifestations of deity "were too fair to worship, too divine to love". But in the person of Christ it is the reverse that was true: "He came unto His own." A sanctifier must be one with those whom He sanctifies. The very separateness in character between the two parties makes it necessary that in some way they should be one. There must be a point of contact, one with the other. He who is like his brethren will have more power over them than one who is not like them. Hence, in order to be a sanctifier, Our Blessed Lord had to be a man like His unholy brethren. He would make them holy by reproducing in His life the lost ideal of human character and bringing that ideal to bear on their minds and hearts.

3

Grace and Faith in Christian Life

Grace is life—the life of God among men. It is that divine life which Christ as the Son of God brought to this earth. It is not something which cuts an unexpected tangent across the harmony of the universe, but rather it is that which perfects the universe in its highest earthly expression, viz.: man.

A treatise on grace might be called a supernatural biology, for the laws of organic life are feeble reflections of the laws of the life of grace. The very notion of biogenesis, the law that all life must come from previous life and can never be spontaneously generated, is a natural truth which should prepare the mind for the supernatural truth that human life can never generate divine life, but that divine life must be a gift. Only life can give life, and only life can come from life. *Omne vivum ex vivo* is as true of supernatural biogenesis as it is of the natural. The life of God, which is grace, is a pure gift of God to which we have no right whatever. It was given to man in the first Adam and restored to man by the merits of the second Adam, Jesus Christ.

The whole order of creation affords us an analogy of the gift quality of grace. If a stone, say the rock of Gibraltar, should suddenly break out into bloom, it would be something transcending its nature. If a rose one day would become conscious and see and feel and touch, it would be a *supra*natural act—an act totally undue to the nature of the rose as such. If an animal would break out into a reasoning process and speak words of wisdom, it would be a supranatural act, for it is not in the nature of an animal to be rational. So too, but in a far more rigorous manner, if man, who by nature is a creature of God, becomes a child of God and a member of the family of the Trinity, and a brother of Jesus Christ, it is a *super*natural act for man, and a gift which surpasses all the exigencies and powers of his nature, even more than blooming surpasses the nature and powers of marble.

Grace makes man more than a "new creature", and infinitely higher than his former condition, than an animal would be if it spoke with the wisdom of Socrates. There is nothing in all creation like that gift by which God calls man a son, and man calls God "Father". The difference between mere human life and human life rendered deiform by grace is not one of development, but of generation. The source of life in both cases is as different as human and divine paternity. The distance which separates some minerals from the vegetable kingdom may be only a hair's breadth—but the distance which separates human life and divine life is infinite. "No one can pass from thence hence."

The world, in the eyes of God, is divided into two classes, the sons of men and the sons of God. All are called to be sons of God, but not all accept the gift worthily, believing that if they should take Christ as their portion, they would have naught else beside. It is to forget that the whole contains the parts, and that in perfect life we have the joys of finite life in an infinite degree.

Both types of sons are born, the one according to the flesh, the other according to the spirit. "That which is born of the flesh is flesh; that which is born of the Spirit

is spirit." Being born of the flesh incorporates us into the
life of Adam; being born of the spirit—of water and of
the Holy Ghost—incorporates us into the life of Christ.
The sons of God are twice born; the sons of men are once
born. The true renaissance is in the sons of God who are
reborn, not by entering again into their mothers' wombs,
"for the flesh profiteth nothing", but by being born of
God, becoming thereby His children and His heirs.

The sons of God are in virtue of their sonship heirs of
heaven; they pass into their heritage at death. The sons
of men are heirs only of riches which rust consumes,
moths eat, and thieves break through and steal. The sons
of God have within themselves the seed of glory and eternal happiness, but not so with the children of men. There
is more difference between two souls on this earth; one in
the state of grace, and the other not in that state, than there
is between two souls, one in the state of grace in this life,
and the other enjoying the eternal blessedness of heaven.
The reason is that grace is the germ of glory and some day
will blossom into glory just as the acorn some day will
become the oak.[1] But the soul not possessed with grace has
no such potencies in it. "Dearly beloved," says St. John,
"we are now the sons of God; and it hath not yet appeared
what we shall be. We know that when He shall appear,
we shall be like unto Him; because we shall see Him as He
is" (1 Jn 3:2).

One wonders why a world so much given to the philosophy of evolution does not see the grace of Jesus Christ
as the answer to its aspirations. One of the reasons why
evolution is held so highly is because of the promise it
gives for the future, and yet, all that it can give, even in its

---

[1] Gratia nihil aliud est quam quaedam inchoatio gloriae aeternae. *Summa*
2–2, q. 24, art. 3 ad 2.

wildest form, is the unfolding of something beneath man. But here in supernatural biology, there is the promise and the potency of a glory for man which exceeds even his imagination—the potency not of becoming a superman, but a son of God. There is no emergent in the whole field of evolution comparable to the "new creatures" which emerge from the Sacrament of Baptism. True greatness of life is not a push from below, but a gift from above: "I am come that you may have life and that in abundance."

It is possible for a man to live on one of three levels. The first level is the subhuman, or the animal, in which a man is content to live only for his body, for his flesh and its pleasures; when a whole society lives thus, we have what Sorokin has called a "sensate culture". If reason is used at all on this lowest level, it is only to discover new techniques for providing thrills and amusements for the animal nature. Man can also live on a second, or higher, level, the rational; here he will pursue a good pagan life and will defend the natural virtues, but without great enthusiasm. Under the inspiration of reason alone, he is tolerant, philanthropic; he favors the underdog and contributes to community enterprises, but he refuses to believe that there is a knowledge beyond the reach of his own intellect or a strength exceeding his own will. For high above these two levels there is a third, which is the divine level; in this, man, thanks to the grace of God, is elevated to the supernatural order and is made a child of God.

These three levels might be compared to a three-story house: the first floor is hardly furnished at all; the second has some comforts; but the third is orderly, luxurious, and full of peace. An individual who lives for purely animal pleasures will take as sheer nonsense the suggestion that there is a level of reason above the first floor, where he lives according to his lusts. And to suggest to those who live on the second floor of reason that there is still a floor above, where peace of mind becomes peace of soul, is to invite them to ridicule the supernatural order. Those who dwell on the second floor have no understanding whatever of the supernatural; they regard it as a pious extra, as unessential as frost on a windowpane or frosting on a cake. They are willing to admit that there is assimilation in the universe and that the progress has been upward and vertical from the chemical to man, but when it comes to the development of man himself, they refuse to admit a continuation of the same vertical process. They see the past in terms of an upward process until man was produced; from that time on, they insist that it moves only on a horizontal plane and that man's progress is to be measured by his growing skill in the manipulation of nature and wealth and the acquiring of better material conditions—all of which are external to man. Those who refuse to mount to the third floor from the second are much like the two tadpoles who were one day discussing the possibility of a realm higher than that of the tadpoles. One little tadpole said to the other, "I think I will stick my head above the water to see what the rest of the world looks like." The other tadpole said, "Don't be foolish. You don't mean to tell me that there is anything in this world besides water!"

A reasonable being should ask himself why—if chemicals can enter into plants, and plants be taken up into animals, and animals be taken into man—why man himself, who is the peak of visible creation, should be denied the privilege of being assimilated into higher power? The rose has no right to say that there is no life above it—and neither has man, who has a vast capacity and unconquerable yearning for eternal life and truth and love.

The supernatural, the third level on which we may live, is not an outgrowth of the natural, as the oak develops from an acorn. It marks a complete break, a beginning anew. The development is not a gradual progress, in which a man becomes more tolerant, more broad-minded, more articulate about social justice, less hateful and less avaricious, until finally he reaches a point where he finds himself a Christian and a citizen of the supernatural order. That is not the way it happens.

It is a law of physics that a body continues in a state of rest or uniform motion in a straight line until it is compelled by outside forces to change that state; man, too, is subject to inertia, and he will remain in a merely natural state unless he is changed from the outside. Stones do not become elephants, nor elephants men. Man, by nature, is only a creature of God, almost as a stone or a bird is a creature of God—although man reflects some of the attributes of the Creator more faithfully than the stars and the plants do. In truth, the supernatural order is something to which man is not entitled; nevertheless it once belonged to our race. As a result, every man is now a king in exile. But the supernatural privilege of being a child of God, entitled to call Him Father, was always as unattainable to the nature of man as life is to a crystal.

How does man enter into this higher, divine life? The answer is simple: we must follow what would appear to be a universal law. While preserving a complete distinction between nature and grace, we must follow the same law the mineral follows in entering into the plant life, and the plant in entering into the animal life, namely, *we must die to ourselves*. Before the plant can live in the animal it must be torn up from its roots and pass, in a certain sense, through the jaws of death; before the animal can enter into the life of man it must pass through fire and water which constitute its Gethsemane and its Calvary. Each thing must die to itself, it must immolate itself if it is to have its life perfected. Nothing is "born" to a higher life unless it be born "from above". If the plant could speak it would say to the mineral: "Unless you are born again, you cannot enter into my kingdom." If the animal could speak it would say to the plants and the minerals: "Unless you are born again, you cannot enter into my kingdom." These elevations bear a remote and imperfect analogy to our own life. Yet Christ can speak for He is the Word; He can say to man, "Unless a man be born again of water and the Holy Spirit, he cannot enter into the Kingdom of God." And that being "born again" is Baptism. Plunged in the regenerating waters of that sacrament, we die to our natural lives and begin to live spiritual lives, not as creatures, but as very children in the family of the Trinity, whereby we have the right to call God "Father". As the plant dies and is buried to its plant life, so too, in a more eminent way "we are buried together with Christ by baptism unto death, that as Christ is risen from the dead by the glory of the Father, so we also may walk in the newness of life" (Rom 6:4).

The divine life of grace is communicated to us principally through the sacraments. Our whole social life is intertwined with "sacraments" in the broad sense of the term, inasmuch as what they hold they hide, and they bring what they veil. The clasping of hands, the kiss—we do not chafe at them, or should not. A kiss may be a poor way of expressing and indeed conveying love; even by a kiss we may betray, as Judas did. Yet true lovers do not feel their kiss divides them, comes between them, or caricatures their love simply because it is physical and external. It is an expression of what they feel in their hearts. Now, the sacraments are the kiss of God where He not only pours out the riches of His love, but satisfies the hungers of the senses and thought as well as the soul.

The sacraments are the communication of the life of God. And there is a parallel between the physical and the spiritual life. What elements are necessary for our physical life? Are there not five for the individual physical life and two for our social life? As individuals, first, we must be born; second, we must grow; third, we must nourish ourselves; fourth, we must heal our wounds; and fifth, drive out all traces of infirmity and disease. As social beings, first, we must have order and government; and second, we must pass on our life to posterity. These seven elements are required in the spiritual order and the seven make up the seven sacraments. First, we must be born: that is Baptism; second, we must grow spiritually and reach the stage of Christian virility: that is Confirmation; third, we must nourish our souls on the Bread of Life: that is the Eucharist; fourth, we must bind up our spiritual wounds: that is Penance; fifth, we must root out all traces of spiritual infirmities: that is Extreme Unction. But we are also social beings. We need government and a source of unity and the priesthood: that is Holy Orders. We need to continue the existence of the race: that is Matrimony.

Thus the spiritual life is a perfection of the physical life and the seven sacraments instituted by Christ are so many channels of that divine life whose reservoir is Calvary.

"We approach, and in spite of the darkness, our hands, or our head, or our brow, or our lips become, as it were, sensible of the contact of something more than earthly. We know not where we are, but we have been bathing in water and a voice tells us that it is blood. Or we have a mark signed upon our foreheads and it spake of Calvary. Or we recollect a hand laid upon our heads and surely it had the print of the nails upon it and resembled His who with a touch gave sight to the blind and raised the dead. Or we have been eating or drinking; and it was not a dream surely that One fed us from His wounded side, and renewed our nature by the heavenly meat He gave."[2]

Take Baptism for example. Baptism is not an arbitrary ritual; it is a law of life, a special law of the supernatural order, it is true, but a law nevertheless. God might have used some other means to effect our incorporation into His life, but certainly the means He has chosen are consonant with the whole order in which nature works. The necessity of Baptism as a means of eternal salvation then is of divine origin. It was Jesus Christ Himself who told us so. But it is not just a command for the mere sake of making a ritual, as some in the modern world would have us believe. Looking back from its revelation to nature, we can see all nature crying out the necessity of Baptism in the sense that it demands a death as a condition of rebirth. This process of dying in order to live which is initiated in us by Baptism must be continued throughout the whole Christian life, and continued throughout the whole Christian life it is mortification. It is one of the aspects of the metabolic processes of the Christian life.

"Unless the grain of wheat falling to the ground die, itself remaineth alone." The power to find life through death makes the seed nobler than the diamond. In falling to the ground it loses its outer envelope which is a restraining power of the life within it. But once this outer skin dies in the ground, then life pushes forth into the blade. So too, unless we die to the world with its vices and its concupiscences, we shall not spring forth into life everlasting. If we are to live in a higher life, we must die to the lower life; if we live in the lower life of this world, we die to a higher life which is Christ. To put the whole law

---

[2] John Henry Newman, *Parochial and Plain Sermons*, bk. 5, no. 1 (San Francisco: Ignatius Press, 1997), 965.

in the beautiful paradox of Our Divine Lord: if we wish to save our life, we must lose it, that is, if we wish to save it for eternity, we must lose it for time; if we wish to save it for the Father's mansions, we must lose it for this dull world; if we wish to save it for perfect happiness, we must lose it for fleeting pleasure of mortality.

> The fall doth pass the rise in worth;
> For birth hath in itself the germ of death,
> But death hath in itself the germ of birth.
> It is the falling acorn buds the tree,
> The falling rain that bears the greenery,
> The fern-plants moulder when the ferns arise.
> For there is nothing lives but something dies,
> And there is nothing dies but something lives,
>   Till skies be fugitives,
> Till Time, the hidden root of change, updries
> Are Birth and Death inseparable on earth;
> For they are twain yet one, and Death is Birth.[3]

What does the soul feel like when it begins to encounter the grace of God?

1. The soul feels itself in a crisis. On the one hand there is a profound sense of one's own helplessness and, on the other hand, by an equally certain conviction that God alone can supply what the individual lacks. If there were *only* a sense of helplessness, there would be despair, pessimism, and eventual suicide. This is, indeed, the condition of the post-Christian pagan: he feels the total inadequacy of his own inner resources against the overwhelming odds of a cruel universe and thus falls into despair. He has one-half of the necessary condition for conversion—namely,

---

[3] Francis Thompson, "Ode to the Setting Sun" (1897).

a sense of crisis—but he fails to link up his powerlessness with the divine power, Who sustains and nourishes the soul. But when this is done, paganism vanishes and gives place to what might be called creative despair: "despair", because one realizes his own spiritual disease; "creative", because he knows that only a divine physician outside himself can bring healing to his wings. This despair does not usually arise from a sense of one's stupidity or ignorance or mistakes, but because of one's inadequacy, one's sense of dependence, or even one's admission of guilt.

2. The soul becomes the battlefield of a civil war during a conversion. It is not enough that there be a conflict between consciousness and unconsciousness or self and environment, for such tensions can be simply psychological. The tension or conflict is never very acute when the dueling forces are contained within the mind itself; conversion is not autosuggestion, but a flash of lightning from without. There is a great tension only when the self is confronted with the nonself, when the within is challenged by the without, when the helplessness of the ego is confronted with the adequacy of the divine.

Not until the tug of war begins, with the soul on one end of the rope and God on the other, does true duality appear as the condition of conversion. There must be in the soul the conviction that one is in the grip of and swayed by a higher control than one's own will; that, opposing the ego, there is a presence before whom one feels happy in doing good and before whom one shrinks away for having done evil. It is relatively unimportant whether this crisis, which results in a feeling of duality, be sudden or gradual. What matters is struggle between the soul and God, with the all-powerful God never destroying human freedom. This is the greatest drama of existence.

3. There is an impression that one is being sought by someone—by the "Hound of Heaven" in Thompson's

language—who will not leave us alone. The tragedy is that many souls, feeling this anxiety, seek to have it explained away, instead of following it to where, at the end of the trail, it is seen as God and actual grace working on the soul. The voice of God causes discontent within the soul in order that the soul may search further and be saved. It embarrasses the soul, for it shows us the truth, tears off all the masks and masquerades of hypocrisy. But it consoles the soul, too, by effecting a harmony with self, with fellow man, and with God. It is for man to decide—to accept or reject the voice he hears. Once these two currents of inner frustration and divine mercy meet, so that the soul realizes that God alone can provide what it lacks, then the crisis reaches a point where a decision must be made. In this sense, the crisis is crucial—it involves a cross. The crisis itself can take a thousand different forms, varying from souls which are good to those which are sinful. But in both these extremes there is a common recognition that the conflicts and frustrations cannot be overcome by one's own energy. The common forms of crisis are the moral, the spiritual, and the physical.

4. The soul now wants to get out of its sins.

Up to this point, the soul had covered up its sins; now it discovers them in order to repudiate them. What is owned can be disowned; what is perceived as an obstacle can now be surmounted. The crisis reaches its peak when the soul becomes less interested in stirring up external revolutions and more interested in the internal revolution of its own spirit; when it swings swords, not outward but inward, to cut out its baser passions; when it complains less about the lying of the world and begins to work on making itself less a liar than before. The moral sphere has two ethical poles: one, the immanent sense of evil or failure; the other, the transcendent power of God's mercy. The abyss of powerlessness cries out to the abyss of salvation, for *copiosa apud eum redemptio.* The Cross is now seen in a new light. At one moment, it bespeaks the depth of human iniquity which, in essence, would slay God; at another moment it reveals the defeat of evil in its strongest moment, vanquished not only by the prayers for forgiveness from the Cross but by the triumph of the Resurrection. But this cascade of divine power cannot operate on a man so long as he lives under the illusion either that he is an angel or that sin is not his fault. He must first admit the fact of personal guilt; then—though the consciousness of having been a sinner does not vanish—the consciousness of being in a state of sin is relieved. This is probably the experience to which Charles Péguy referred when he said, "I am a sinner, a good sinner."

Once the will to sin is abandoned, then the soul sees that it has become acceptable to the Savior—not because it was good, but because the Savior is Good. In other religions, one must be purified before he can knock at the door; in Christianity, one knocks on the door as a sinner, and He Who answers to us heals. The moral crisis is ended when Christ confronts the soul, not as law but as mercy, and when the soul accepts the invitation, "Come to me, all you that labor, and are burdened, and I will refresh you" (Mt 11:28).

5. There is a definite change in behavior and conduct of life. Not only does conversion change one's values; it also reverses the tendencies and energies of life, directing them to another end. If the convert before conversion was already leading a good moral life, there is now less emphasis on keeping a law and more emphasis on maintaining a relationship of love. If the convert has been a sinner, his spiritual life frees him from habits and excesses which before weighed down the soul. He no longer need resort to alcohol or sleeping tablets. He often finds that these

practices were not so much appetites as attempts to flee
responsibility or to ensure, by plunging into unconsciousness, that he could avoid the necessity of choice. Before
conversion, it was behavior which to a large extent determined belief; after conversion, it is belief which determines behavior. There is no longer a tendency to find
scapegoats to blame for the faults of self, but rather a consciousness that the reformation of the world must begin
with the reformation of self. There is still a fear of God,
but it is not the servile fear a subject has for a dictator, but
a filial fear, such as a loving son has for a good father
whom he would never wish to hurt. From such a Love
one does not ever need to run away, and the previous acts
of dissipation, which were disguised forms of flight, are
now renounced.

Once the soul has turned to God, there is no longer
a struggle to give up these habits; they are not so much
defeated, as crowded out by new interests. There is no
longer a need of escape—for one is no longer in flight
from himself. He who once did his own will now seeks
to do God's will; he who once served sin now hates it; he
who once found thoughts of God dry or even unpleas-
ant now hopes above all else one day to behold the God
Whom he loves. The transition the soul has undergone is
as unmistakable as the passage from death to life; there has
been, not a mere giving up of sin, but such a surrender
to divine love as makes him shrink from sin because he
would not wound the Divine Beloved.

6. The soul also receives *certitude*. Philosophy gives a
proof for the existence of God; the science of apologetics
gives the motives for believing in Christ, the Son of God;
but all the incontrovertible proofs they offer fall short of
the certitude that actually comes to a convert through the
gift of faith. Imagine a young man whose father has been

lost for years. A friend, returned from a trip, assures him that he has certain evidence that his father really exists on another continent. But the young man is not fully satisfied with the evidence, however convincing it is; until he is restored to his father's actual presence, he will not have peace. So it is with conversion: before, one knows *about* God; afterward, one *knows* God. The first knowledge the mind has is notional and abstract; the second is real, concrete, and it becomes bound up with all one's sentiments, emotions, passions, and habits. Before conversion, the truths seemed true but far off; they did not touch one personally. After conversion, they become so personalized that the mind knows that it is through with the search for a place to live; it can now settle down to the making of a home. The convert's certitude is so great that his mind does not feel that *an* answer has been given, but *the* answer—the absolute, final solution, which one would die for rather than surrender.

Those who have never gone through the experience of a complete conversion imagine that reason must be completely abdicated for such a step. We hear them make such remarks as, "I cannot understand it; he seemed like an intelligent man." But those who have gone through the experience of conversion see that just as the eye winks, closing itself to the light for an instant that it may reopen and see better, so, too, one winks his reason for that brief instant in which he admits that it may not know *all* the answers. Then, when faith comes, the reason is found to be intact and clearer sighted than before. Both reason and faith are now seen as deriving from God Himself; they can never, therefore, be in opposition. Knowing this, the convert loses all his doubts. His certitude in his faith becomes unshakable—indeed, it is his old notions which are now apt to be shaken by the earthquake of his faith.

7. Another effect is: *peace of soul*. There is a world of difference between peace of mind and peace of soul. Peace of mind is the result of bringing *some* ordering principle to bear on discordant human experiences; this may be achieved by tolerance, or by a gritting of one's teeth in the face of pain; by killing conscience, or denying guilt, or by finding new loves to assuage old griefs.

The peaceful soul does not seek, now, to live morally, but to live for God; morality is only a by-product of the union with Him. This peace unites the soul with his neighbor, prompting him to visit the sick, to feed the hungry, and to bury the dead.

All the energy that was previously wasted in conflict—either in trying to find the purpose of life or in trying alone and futilely to conquer his vices—can now be released to serve a single purpose. Regret, remorse, fears, and the anxieties that flowed from sin now completely vanish in repentance. The convert no longer regrets what he might have been; the Holy Spirit fills his soul with a constant presentiment of what he can become through grace. This spiritual recuperation is accompanied by hope, at no matter what age the change occurs—although the convert always regrets that he waited so long. As St. Augustine said, "Too late, O ancient beauty, have I loved Thee." But since grace rejuvenates, it quickens even the old to consecrated service.

And there are many other ways in which peace of soul will manifest itself after conversion: it makes somebodies out of nobodies by giving them a service of divine sonship; it roots out anger, resentments, and hate by overcoming sin; it gives the convert faith in other people, whom he now sees as potential sons of God; it improves his health by curing the ills that sprang from a disordered, unhappy, and restless mind; for trials and difficulties, it gives him

the aid of divine power; it brings him at all times a sense
of harmony with the universe; it sublimates his passions;
it makes him fret less about the spiritual shortcomings of
the world because he is engrossed in seeking his own
spiritualization; it enables the soul to live in a constant
consciousness of God's presence, as the earth, in its flight
about the sun, carries its own atmosphere with it. In business, in the home, in household duties, in the factory, all
actions are done in the sight of God, all thoughts revolve
about His truths. The unreasoning blame, the false accusations, the jealousies and bitterness of others are borne
patiently, as our Lord bore them, so that love might reign
and that God might be glorified in the bitter as in the
sweet. Dependence on Him becomes strength; one no
longer fears to undertake good works, knowing He will
supply the means. But above all else, with this deep sense
of peace, there is the gift of perseverance, which inspires
us never to let down our guard, or to shrink from difficulties, or to be depressed as the soul presses on to its supernal
vocation in Christ Jesus, Our Lord.

Regardless of your religious background, you have doubt-
less observed the tremendous disparity of points of view
between those who possess divine faith through God's grace
and those who have it not. Have you ever noticed when
discussing important subjects, as pain, sorrow, sin, happiness, marriage, children, education, the purpose of life, and
the meaning of death, that the Catholic point of view is
now poles apart from what is called the modern view?
    You who have the faith probably have often felt a sense
of inadequacy in dealing with those who have no faith,
as if there were no common denominator. You and that
person without faith seem to be living in different worlds.
You feel powerless to penetrate the natural mentality of

the modern pagan whom you meet on the street. It is like telling a blind man about color. You are not talking the same language. As with workmen on the Tower of Babel, there is no common understanding.

It was not so many years ago that those who rejected many Christian truths were considered off the reservation; e.g., the divorced who remarried, the atheists, the enemies of the family, or those who held that law was a dictate of the will, not of reason. Today, it is we who are considered off the reservation. It is they who are on it. The Christian is today on the defensive if for no other reason than because he is the exception.

The clarity of vision and certitude of those who have the gift of faith is sometimes misunderstood even by those who have faith. Hence a Catholic is sometimes impatient with one who has not the faith, wrongly thinking that the reason he sees the truth so clearly is because of his own innate cleverness, and the reason his neighbor does not see it is due either to his stupidity or his stubbornness. Faith, it must be remembered, is not due to our wisdom, and the lack of faith is not due to their ignorance. Faith is solely a gift of God. "Flesh and blood hath not revealed it to thee, but my Father who is in heaven" (Mt 16:17).

If you have not the faith, have you not often considered as utterly foolish, absurd, and superstitious the judgments, the philosophy of life, and the outlook of those who live by faith? You think a Catholic, for instance, has surrendered both his freedom and his reason by obeying the laws of the Church and by accepting the truth of Christ in His Church.

Your judgment, then, is very much like one who looks at the windows of a church from outside, where they seem to be a meaningless confusion of leaden lines and dull colors. Once inside the church, and the leaden lines fade away as the pattern reveals itself vibrant with colors and life. In like manner, the Church may seem bewildering to those who are outside, but once you enter it, you will discover an order and harmony and a "beauty that leaves all other beauty plain".

The world today seems much more united in its negation of belief than in its acceptance of a belief. The older generation could give you at least ten reasons for a wrong belief, such as a belief in materialism, but the modern man cannot give even one bad reason for total unbelief.

It is shockingly true that there is more in common today between a Christian in the state of grace, and a Buddhist or Orthodox Jew or a Moslem than there is between the true Christian and the average so-called Christian person you are apt to meet at a night club, or even at the table in your neighbor's house.

When the Christian talks about God, the Buddhist or Orthodox Jew or Moslem can understand him, for they, too, believe that God is sovereign and judge of all men. But to the average pagan who believes man came from beast and, therefore, must act like one, all this is as so much fatuous nonsense and senile stupidity. A striking confirmation of this is that in the face of anti-God crusades of Russia, Christians, Jews, and Moslems presented a common front.

Why this difference between those who have the faith, and those who have it not? It is due to the fact that a soul in the state of grace has its intellect illumined, which enables it to perceive new truths which otherwise would be beyond its powers. Divine grace supernaturalizes that which makes us human, namely, our intellect and our will, giving them the power of higher action. The intellect still continues to know truth, but through grace operating in it as faith, it knows higher truths than those of reason. The human will in like manner retains its love of good, but by grace operating on it, it can now rely more on God or love Him more than by its unaided efforts.

You have exactly the same eyes at night as you have in the day, but you cannot see at night, because you lack the additional light of the sun. So, too, let two minds with identically the same education, the same mental capacities, and the same judgment, look on a Host enthroned on an altar. The one sees bread, the other sees Christ, not, of course, with the eyes of the flesh, but with the eyes of faith. Let them both look on death: one sees the end of a biological entity, the other an immortal creature being judged by God on how it used its freedom. The reason for the difference is: one has a light which the other lacks, namely, the light of faith.

This light of faith operates on human problems somewhat like an X ray. You look at a box with the naked eye and it appears to be of wood and tinsel and cheap wrapping paper, and, therefore, of no great value. You look at it later with an X ray and you see the contents of the box to be diamonds and rubies. In like manner, those who live only by the light of reason gaze upon a sick and feverish body, and see pain as valueless as a curse. But the mind endowed with the extra light of faith sees through the pain: to him it is either a means for reparation for sins, or a stepping stone to greater unity with his master, whom "life made love, and love made pain, and pain made death".

If you have not the light of faith, you may be very educated, but can you correlate your knowledge into a unified philosophy of life? Does your psychology jibe with your ethics? Does your emphasis on the dignity of man click with your denial of a soul? Rather is not your mind like a flattened Japanese lantern, a riot of colors without pattern or purpose? What you need to do is to have the candle of faith lighted on the inside of that lantern that you may see all your different lines of knowledge meet into one absorbing pattern leading to God.

Education is not the condition of receiving this additional light of faith, although an educated person can understand the faith better. Since the light of faith is from God and not from us, we cannot supply it, any more than we can restore vision if we lose our eyes. Being a true Christian, therefore, does not require an education. *It is an education!*

A little child who today is telling a Sister in school that God made him, that he was made to know, love, and serve God, and to be happy with Him in the next world, knows more, and is more profoundly educated, than all the professors throughout the length and breadth of this land who babble about space-time deities, who prattle about new ethics to fit unethical lives, who negate all morality to suit their unmoral thinking, but who do not know, therefore, that beyond time is the timeless, beyond space is the spaceless, the Infinite Lord and Master of the Universe.

No wonder Our Lord prayed: "I confess to thee, O Father, Lord of heaven and earth, because thou hast hidden these things from the wise and prudent, and hast revealed them to little ones. Yea, Father, for so it hath seemed good in thy sight" (Lk 10:21). St. Paul later on clearly distinguished between these two kinds of wisdom: the false wisdom which uses reason to negate the God who gave reason, and the higher wisdom born of the grace of God: "For the foolishness of God is wiser than men; and the weakness of God is stronger than men" (1 Cor 1:25).

That is why those who live by the higher light of faith are so insistent that education be religious, for, after all, if one does not know *why* he is living, there is not much purpose in living. There are those who would suggest that there be no religious training until the child is old enough to "decide for himself". They should also consistently suggest a child in a slum should not be removed to a better environment until he is old enough to decide for himself. Unfortunately, when that time comes he may already have contracted tuberculosis. Why not also argue that no infant should be born into the world until he is old enough to decide who his parents should be, to what economic class he will belong, and to what code he will subscribe, or even to decide whether he wants to come into the world at all.

Though faith is a gift of God, and though God will give it to those that ask it, there is one very human obstacle why more minds do not receive it, and that is pride. Pride is the commonest sin of the modern mind, and yet the one of which the modern mind is never conscious. You have heard people say: "I like drink too much", or "I am quick tempered", but did you ever hear anyone say: "I am conceited"?

Pride is the exaltation of self as an absolute standard of truth, goodness, and morality. It judges everything by itself, and for that reason everyone else is a rival, particularly God. Pride makes it impossible to know God. If I know everything, then not even God can teach me anything. If I am filled with myself, then there is no place for God. Like the inns of Bethlehem, we say to the divine visitor: "There is no room."

Pride is of two kinds: it is either the pride of omniscience or the pride of nescience. The pride of omniscience tries to convince your neighbor you know everything; the new pride of nescience tries to convince your neighbor that he knows nothing. The latter is the technique used by "sophomores" who pride themselves on the fact that man can know nothing. Hence, they doubt everything, and of this they are very sure. They seem to forget that the doubting of everything is impossible, for doubt is a shadow, and there can be no shadow without light.

If pride is the great human obstacle to faith, it follows that, from the human side, the essential condition of receiving faith is humility. Humility is not an underestimation of what we are, but the plain, unadulterated truth. A man who is six feet tall is not humble if he says: "No, really, I am only five feet tall."

If there ever came a moment in your life when you admitted you did not know it all, or said: "Oh! What a fool am I", you created a vacuum and a void which God's grace could fill. Before you accept the gift of faith, there may be a moment when you will think that you are giving up your reason; but that is only seeming, not real.

As the blink of the eye is the condition of better vision, so with your reason in relation to faith. There comes a time in conversion when you blink on your reason, that is, you doubt about its capacity to know everything, and you affirm the possibility that God could enlighten you. Then comes the gift of faith. Once that is received, you find out that instead of destroying your reason, you have perfected it. Faith now becomes to your reason what a telescope is to your eye; it opens up new fields of vision and new worlds which before were hidden and unknown.

Think not either that you lose your freedom by accepting the faith. A few years ago, I received a letter from a radio listener who said: "I imagine that you from your earliest youth were surrounded by priests and nuns who never permitted you to think for yourself. Why not throw off the yoke of Rome and begin to be free?"

I answered him thus: "In the center of a sea was an island on which children played and danced and sang. Around that island were great high walls which had stood for centuries. One day, some strange men came to the island in individual rowboats, and said to the children: Who put up these walls? Can you not see that they are destroying your freedom? Tear them down!

"The children tore them down! Now if you go there, you will find all the children huddled together in the center of the island, afraid to play, afraid to sing, afraid to dance—afraid of falling into the sea."

Faith is not a dam which prevents the flow of the river of reason and thought; it is a levee which prevents unreason from flooding the countryside. Our senses were meant by God to be perfected by reason. That is why a man who loses his reason deliberately by drunkenness no longer sees as well as an animal, nor behaves as well as an animal. We say: "He has lost his senses."

Once the human senses have been deprived of reason, which is their perfection, they no longer function even as well as the sense of an animal. In like manner, once the human reason has lost faith, which is the perfection God freely intended it to have, then reason does not function as well without faith as it does with it. That is why reason alone is unable to get us out of the mess we are in today. Of and by itself, it cannot function well enough to handle the problems created by loss of faith and by misuse of reason and sin.

The following facts about faith are important:

1. Faith is not believing that something will happen, nor is it the acceptance of what is contrary to reason, nor is it an intellectual recognition which a man might give to something he does not understand or which his reason cannot prove, e.g., relativity. Faith is the acceptance of a truth on the authority of God revealing.

Faith is a supernatural virtue, whereby, inspired and assisted by the grace of God, we believe as true those things which He revealed, not because the truth of these things is clearly evident from reason alone, but because of the authority of God Who cannot deceive nor be deceived.

Before faith, one makes an investigation by reason. Just as no business man would extend you credit without a reason for doing so, neither are you expected to put faith in anyone without a reason. Before you have faith, you study the motives of believing, e.g., Why should I put faith in Christ?

Your reason investigates the miracles He worked, the prophecies which pre-announced Him, and the consonance of His teaching with your reason. These constitute the preambles of faith, from which you form a judgment of credibility: "This truth, that Christ is the Son of God, is worthy of belief." Passing to the practical order, you add: "I must believe it."

From then on, you give your assent: "I believe He is the Son of God, and this being so, whatever He reveals, I will accept as God's truth." The motive for your assent in faith is always the authority of God, Who tells you it is true. You would not believe unless you saw that you must believe.

You believe the truths of reason because there is intrinsic evidence; you believe in the truths of God because there is extrinsic evidence. You believe the sun is ninety-three million miles away from the earth though you never measured it; you believe that Moscow is the capital of Russia, though you never saw it. So you accept the truths of Christianity on the authority of God revealed in His Son Jesus Christ, Our Lord.

Faith, therefore, never is blind. Since your reason is dependent on uncreated reason or divine truth, it follows that your reason should bow down to what God reveals. You believe now, not because of the arguments; they were only a necessary preliminary. You believe because God said it. The torch now burns by its own brilliance.

The nature of the act of faith was revealed by Our Lord's attitude toward the unbelieving Pharisees. They had seen miracles worked and prophecies fulfilled. They were not lacking in motives for belief. But they still refused to believe. Our Lord took a little child in His midst and said: "Amen I say to you, whosoever shall not receive the kingdom of God as a little child, shall not enter into it" (Mk 10:15).

By this He meant that the act of faith has more in common with the trusting belief of a child in his mother, than with the assent of a critic. The child believes what the mother tells him because she said it. His belief is an unaffected and trusting homage of love to his mother.

When the Christian believes, he does so, not because he has in the back of his mind the miracles of Christ, but because of the authority of One Who can neither deceive nor be deceived. "If we receive the testimony of men, the testimony of God is greater. For this is the testimony of God, which is greater, because He hath testified of His Son. He that believeth in the Son of God, hath the testimony of God in himself. He that believeth not the Son, maketh him a liar; because he believeth not in the testimony which God hath testified of His Son" (1 Jn 5:9–10).

2. You cannot argue or study or reason or hypnotize or whip yourself into faith. Faith is a gift of God. When anyone instructs you in Christian doctrine, he does not give you faith. He is only a spiritual agriculturist, tilling the soil of your soul, uprooting a few weeds and breaking up the clods of egotism. It is God Who drops the seed. "For by grace you are saved through faith, and that not of yourselves, for it is the gift of God" (Eph 2:8).

If faith were a will to believe, you could produce your own faith by an act of the will. All you can do is to dispose yourself for its reception from the hands of God. As a dry stick is better disposed for burning than a wet stick, so a humble man is better disposed for faith than a know-it-all. In either case, as the fire which burns must come from outside the stick, so your faith must come from outside yourself, namely, from God.

When you try to make everything clear by reason, you somehow only succeed in making everything confusion. Once you introduce a single mystery, everything else becomes clear in the light of that one mystery. The sun is the "mystery" in the universe; it is so bright you cannot look at it; you cannot "see" it. But in the light of it, everything else becomes clear. As Chesterton once said: "But you can see the moon and things under the moon, but the moon is the mother of lunatics."

3. Faith is unique and vital. There are not many faiths. There is only one faith: "One Lord, one faith, one baptism" (Eph 4:5). Out of the millions and millions of men who walked this earth, there is only one who is the Incarnate Lord; out of the millions of lights in the heaven, there is only one sun to light a world. "Upon this rock I will build my Church"—not "my churches".

Faith is like life; it must be taken in its entirety. Two mothers appeared in the court of Solomon. Both claimed a babe as their own. Solomon said that he would divide the child and give each claimant a half. One of the women protested and said: "Give the babe to her." Wise Solomon thereupon decided that the babe belonged to the one who protested, for she was the real mother. The Church is like that: it insists on the whole truth.

Hence, you may not pick and choose among the words of the Blessed Lord and say: "I will accept the Sermon on the Mount, but not Your words about hell." Or, "I believe in Your doctrine of motherhood, but I cannot accept Your teaching that it is unlawful for a man to divorce and marry again." The truths of God are like that babe: it is either the whole babe, or nothing.

Every religion in the world, I care not what it is, contains some reflection of one eternal truth. Every philosophy, every world-religion, every sect, contains an arc of the perfect round of the natural and revealed truth. Confucianism has the fraction of fellowship; Indian asceticism has the fraction of self-abnegation; each human sect has an aspect of Christ's truth.

That is why, in approaching those who have not the faith, one should not begin by pointing out their errors, but rather by indicating the fraction of truth they have in common with the fullness of Truth. Instead of saying to the Confucian: "You are wrong in ignoring the Fatherhood of God", one should say: "You are right in emphasizing brotherhood, but to make your brotherhood perfect, you need the Fatherhood of God and the Sonship of Christ, and the vivifying unity of the Holy Spirit."

So, with every other religion and sect in the world. Today, men are starving. One should not go to them and say: "Do not eat poisons; they will kill you." We need only to give bread. In religion, in like manner, there is too much emphasis on the errors of unbelievers and not enough on the affirmation of truth by believers. Break the bread of affirmation and teaching, and the grace of God will do the rest.

This is the great beauty of the Catholic Faith; its sense of proportion, or balance, or should we say, its humor. It does not handle the problem of death to the exclusion of sin, nor the problem of pain to the exclusion of matter; nor the problem of sin to the exclusion of human freedom, nor the social use of property to the exclusion of personal right, nor the reality of the body and sex to the exclusion of the soul and its function, nor the reality of matter to the forgetfulness of the Spirit.

It never allows one doctrine to go to your head, like wine in an empty stomach. It keeps its balance, for truth is a precarious thing. Like the great rocks in the Alps, there are a thousand angles at which they will fall, but there is only one at which they would stand.

It is easy to be a "pink" in the twentieth century, as it was easy to be a "liberal" in the nineteenth; it is easy to be a "materialist" today, as it was easy to be an "idealist" in the nineteenth century, but to keep one's head in the midst of all these changing moods and fancies, so that one is right, not when the world is right, but right when the world is wrong, is the thrill of a tight-rope walker, the thrill of the romance of orthodoxy.

4. The acceptance of the fullness of truth will have the unfortunate quality of making you hated by the world. Forget for a moment the history of Christianity, and the fact that Christ existed. Suppose there appeared in this world today a man who claimed to be divine truth; and who did not say: "I will teach you truth", but "I am *the Truth*." Suppose he gave evidence by his works of the truth of his statement. Knowing ourselves as we do, with our tendency to relativism, to indifference, and to the fusing of right and wrong, how do you suppose we would react to that divine truth? With hatred, with obloquy, with defiance; with charges of intolerance, narrow mindedness, bigotry, and crucifixion.

That is what happened to Christ. That is what Our Lord said would happen to those who accept His truth. "If you had been of the world, the world would love its own: but because you are not of the world, but I have chosen you out of the world, therefore the world hateth you. Remember my word that I said to you: The servant is not greater than his master. If they have persecuted me they will also persecute you: if they have kept my word, they will keep yours also" (Jn 15:19–20).

Hence I believe that if the grace of God did not give me the fullness of truth, and I were looking for it, I would begin my search by looking through the world for a church that did not get along with the evil in the world! If that church were accused of countless lies, hated because it refused to compromise, ridiculed because it refused to fit the times and not all time, I would suspect that since it was hated by what is evil in the world, it therefore was good and holy; and if it is good and holy, it must be divine. And I would sit down by its fountains and begin to drink the waters of everlasting life.

What will faith do for you?

1. It will preserve your freedom. You still live in a world in which you are free to ask questions. Unless you build up some resistance to the organized propaganda which is more and more falling into the hands of "pinks" and "reds", you will become the prey of their law and their authority, whose very end is the extinction of your liberty.

Our Blessed Lord said "the truth will make you free." Turning His words around, they mean that if you do not know the Truth, you will be enslaved. If you do not know the truth about addition or subtraction, you will not be free to do your bookkeeping; if you do not know that zebras have stripes, you will not be free to draw them. If you do not know the truth of the nature of man, you will not be free to act as a man.

That is why, as men become indifferent to right and wrong, disorder and chaos increase, and the state steps in to organize the chaos by force. Dictatorships arise in such a fashion. Such is the essence of Socialism, the compulsory organization of chaos.

That is why the Church is in full sympathy today with the multitude of people who, stirred by war, at first vaguely and then unyieldingly, believe that had there been the possibility of censuring and correcting the actions of public authority the world would not have been dragged into war.

Hence democracy worthy of the name can have no other meaning than to place the citizen increasingly in a position to hold his own personal opinion, to express it, and even to make it prevail for the common good.

2. Faith will answer the principal problems of your life: Why? Whence? Whither? If you are without faith, you are like a man who has lost his memory and is locked in a dark room waiting for memory to come back. There are a hundred things you can do: scribble on the wallpaper, cut your initials on the floor, and paint the ceiling. But if you are ever to find out why you are there, and where you are going, you will have to enlarge your world beyond space and time. There is a door out of that room. Your reason can find it. But your reason cannot create the light that floods the room, nor the new world in which you move, which is full of signs on the roadway to the City of Peace and eternal beatitude with God.

3. Faith will enlarge your knowledge, for there are many truths beyond the power of reason. You can look at a painting and from it learn something of the technique of the artist, his skill, and his power; but you could look on it from now until the crack of doom and you could never know the inmost thoughts of the artist. If you were to know them, he would have to reveal them to you. In like manner, you can know something of the power and wisdom of God by looking at His universe, but you could never know His thoughts and life unless He told them. His telling of His inner life is what is called revelation.

Why should we go on saying: "I am the only judge; I am the only standard of truth." These statements remind one of the tourist who, passing through one of the galleries of Florence, remarked to the guide: "I don't think much of these pictures." To which the guide answered: "These pictures are not here for your judgment; they are your judges." So, too, your rejection of the truths beyond reason are the judge of your humility, your love of truth, and your knowledge.

4. Faith will preserve your quality. Have you not noticed that as a man ceases to believe in God, he also ceases to believe in man? Have you observed that, if you have worked for or with a person of deep faith in Christ, you have always been treated with gentleness, equality, and charity? You could not point to a single person who truly loves God and is mean to his fellow man.

Have you noticed that as men lose faith in God, they become selfish, immoral, and cruel? On a cosmic scale, as religion decreases, tyranny increases; as men lose faith in Divinity, they lose faith in humanity. Where God is outlawed, there man is subjugated.

In vain will the world seek for equality until it has seen men through the eyes of faith. Faith teaches that all men, however poor or ignorant or crippled, however maimed or ugly or degraded they may be, all bear within themselves the image of God, and have been bought by the precious blood of Jesus Christ. As this truth is forgotten, men are valued only because of what they can *do*, not because of what they *are*.

Since men cannot do things equally well, e.g., play violins, steer a plane, or teach philosophy, or stoke an engine, they are and must remain forever unequal. From the Christian point of view, all may not have the same rights to do certain jobs, because they lack the capacity; e.g., Toscanini had not a right to pitch for the New York Yankees, but all men have the right to a decent, purposeful, and comfortable life in the structure of the community for which God has fitted them, and first and foremost of all, because of what they are: persons made to the image and likeness of God.

The false idea of the superiority of certain races and classes is due to the forgetfulness of the spiritual foundations of equality. We of the Western world have been rightly proud of the fact that we have a civilization superior to others. But we have given the wrong reason for that superiority. We assume that we are superior because we are white. We are not. We are superior because we are Christians. The moment we cease to be Christian, we will revert to the barbarism from which we came.

In like manner, if the black, brown, and yellow races of the world become converted to Christ, they will produce civilization and culture which will surpass ours if we forget Him who truly made us great. It is conceivable, if we could project ourselves a thousand years in the future and then look back in retrospect over those thousand years, that we might see in China the record of a Christian civilization which would make you forget Notre Dame and Chartres.

5. Finally, faith will enable you to possess the "mind of Christ". "For let this mind be in you, which was also in Christ Jesus" (Phil 2:5). Though you must meditate on the earthly life of Our Lord, you should not allow your mind to dwell exclusively on past events, for by faith your minds are lifted upon the temporal and the contemporary to the eternal mind of Christ.

Everything in the universe fits into the larger rhythm of the divine pattern, which is denied to mortal eyes. From now on, you cease trying to find God in creatures, and begin seeing creatures in God and, therefore, all of value, and worthy of your love. In the multitudinous duties of modern life, you will do nothing which you cannot offer to God as a prayer; you will see that personal sanctity influences society more than social action; your sense of values will change.

You will think less of what you can store away, and more about what you can take with you when you die. Your rebellious moods will give way to resignation. Your tendency to discouragement, which was due to pride, will become an additional reason for throwing yourself like a wounded child into the Father's loving arms. You will cease to be an isolationist and begin to draw strength from the fellowship of the saints and the Body of Christ.

You will think of God's love, not as an emotional paternalism, but as an unalterable dedication to goodness, to which you submit even when it hurts. You will be at peace, not only when things go your way, but when they go against you, because whatever happens you accept as God's will. You will rebuke within yourself all immoderate desires, all presumptuous expectations, all ignoble self-indulgence because they bar the way to Him Who is your way, your truth, and your life.

With Paul you will say in the strength of a great faith: "I am sure that neither death, nor life, nor angels, nor principalities, nor powers, nor things present, nor things to come, nor might, nor height, nor depth, nor any other creature, shall be able to separate us from the love of God, which is in Christ Jesus Our Lord" (Rom 8:38–39).

4

Christ's Office as Teacher, King, and Priest

"Give me a man who loves and I will tell him what God is." Such are the words of St. Augustine. Anyone who ever loved craved unity with that which he loved. Thus in marriage the ideal is the unity of two in one flesh; in religion the ideal is to be one with Christ. There is not a single person who loves Our Dear Lord, who does not strive to be united to Him in thought and in desire and even in body and mind. But here is the problem: How be one with Christ?

His earthly life ended over nineteen hundred years ago. Therefore to some He is only a figure Who crossed the stage of history, as did Caesar and Aristotle, and then was seen no more. Such souls believe that the *only way* they can be united with Our Lord, is by reading what someone wrote concerning Him, or by singing hymns in His name, or by listening to a sermon on His life.

It is no wonder that such people soon begin to think of Our Lord as a teacher of ethics, or as a great humanitarian reformer like Buddha or Socrates, for they too also once lived, preached, and edified, and left behind them a beautiful memory. It is only minds with little power of penetration that say Our Dear Lord "was a good man". May I say that this is precisely what Our Lord was not, viz., a good man, because good men do not lie. If He is not what He claimed to be, what His Miracles witnessed, what the Jewish and Gentile prophecies foretold, viz., the Son of the living God—then He is not just a good man. Then He is a liar, a knave, a deceiver, and a charlatan. If He is not the Christ, the Son of the living God, He is the anti-Christ; but He is not just a good man.

Let us try to understand what Our Divine Lord really is. Begin with yourself. Have you ever thought of how wonderfully you have been made; that there is in you something which can be seen and touched, namely, your body whose nature is fleshy; but there is also something invisible about you, namely your mind and soul with its thoughts, its loves, and its desires. Your soul is, in a sense, "incarnate" in a body (the word incarnate, as you know, means in the flesh); that is, your soul animates and unifies your body.

Now consider the person of Our Divine Lord. He is the true Incarnation, not of a soul in a body, but of God in the form of man. There is something visible about Him, namely, His perfect human nature, which can handle tools, pat little children's heads, be thirsty and think and desire like other men. But there is also something invisible about Him, and that is His divinity. His divinity could no more be seen than your soul, though it could be seen working through His human nature, as your soul works through your body. Just as your body and your soul combine to make one person, so in an infinitely more perfect way, His human nature and His divine nature make but one person, the person of Jesus Christ, the Son of the living God, true God and true man.

We are now prepared to reread our Gospels. St. John closes his Gospel with the words that if he had written down all Our Lord had done "the world itself would not be able to contain the books that should be written" (Jn 21:25). This beautiful variety of Our Lord's words and actions, however, can be reduced to three: He taught, He governed, and He sanctified. He taught, because He is teacher; He governed, because He is King; He sanctified, because He is Savior or priest.

First, as teacher, He is truth. Because He is God, He is absolutely divine, infallible Truth. He said: "I am the truth." For the first time in history, truth and personality were identified. Up until then and since, men have always said: "Here is my doctrine; this is my system; follow these rules." But these ideals were outside their personality, just mere abstractions. No man can fall in love with a theory of geometry or a metaphysical proposition. Truth to be loved must be personal, and Our Lord pointed to Himself as the truth. No one else ever taught that He was the personification of truth. Buddha and others gave systems apart from their personalities. But in the person of Our Lord, truth and personality were one. There was no truth apart from Him. He *is* the truth. Hence, those who say "The Beatitudes are the core of His teaching" miss the point. There was nothing recommended or taught outside or beyond Him, for in Him all the scattered ways and systems found their center and their source. Everyone else gave a code, but He is as romantic as love. All truth—philosophic, scientific, artistic, and legal—is in Him. He is wisdom. He is all the arts and all the sciences. He is the university, for all knowledge turns about Him Who is the truth with whom we can fall in love.

Do you really believe that this divine Truth would come to this earth, speak a few words, and allow them to be wafted away by a Galilean breeze? It is absurd to believe that He Who wrote only once in His life, and that was in the sands, and Who never told anyone to write, should have intended that His truth should be available only and exclusively in a few memoranda that were written down by a few followers over twenty years after His death, and were never gathered together in their approved form until three centuries later. Grant that they are inspired and revealed, and I believe it and confess it and read those writings daily; but I still say it is unthinkable that these books which were not written until His Mystical Body was already spread throughout the whole Roman Empire, should be *His only way* of communicating truth. If He did not take some effective guarantee to preserve His truth, which was so sacred that He died for it, then truth did not matter to Him. If He could not prolong His truth, up to this hour, then He is not God. Either that infallible truth of Jesus Christ is living now, available now, or He is not God. Our problem is to find that infallible divine truth. Come, O Christ, not with a dead truth, but with a living, breathing, speaking truth which is the truth of God to lead the world from darkness into the light. Come with it, even though Thou hast to use human nature to communicate it now as Thou didst not then.

Secondly, Our Lord fulfilled the office of king. As King He is the source of authority. There is something else beside His truth that He ought to have communicated, and that is His authority. As the Son of God He said: "All authority in heaven and on earth has been given to me" (Mt 28:18). The winds and the seas obeyed Him, and when Pilate boasted that he had the power to condemn Him (dictators always speak that way), Our Lord reminded him: "Thou wouldst not have any power over me at all, if it had not been given thee from above" (Jn 19:11).

It is absolutely incredible that this power to change the hearts of all nations should have died with Our Lord. We are living in a world where false authorities are claiming our allegiance, where public opinion makes us dizzy; where the power of the state invades all personal rights. Hence we have need of someone to remind the modern Pilates that there is another power from above. We have plenty of authorities to tell us what is right when the world is right; we want a living Christ today who will tell us what is right when the world is wrong. Come, O Christ, with Thy divine authority, make us free, even though Thou hast to use human natures now as Thou didst not use a human nature then.

Thirdly, Our Lord fulfilled the office of priest or redeemer, for He is the author of our sanctification. When Our Blessed Lord was on earth, not only did He lift up limbs long paralyzed with disease and death, and open blind eyes to the light of God's sunshine, but He cleaned souls and purged hearts. As He identified truth and power with His personality, so He identified sanctification. "I am the Life." And by "Life" He did not mean mere physical life, but spiritual, sanctified, divinized life. He came as a link between God and man. Man is unholy; God is holy, and there is nothing in common between the two. But because He is both God and man, therefore He could be mediator between earth and heaven. This is the meaning of Christ the priest, a link between God and man, bringing God to man and man to God.

It is absurd to think that God Who came to this earth to forgive sins, sanctify our souls, and elevate us to a higher life, should have left us to the mercy of a few literary records and a few hymns to attain this divine life. Shall the Magdalens of our streets be denied the forgiveness that came to the woman who entered Simon's house? Shall the frustrated, the bored, the alcoholics, the fearful who are the way they are because of their sins, go on unforgiven because Christ forgot to prolong His forgiving power?

Shall they whose minds are burdened because they cannot be detached from the past, suffer the added agony of thinking that Christ is past and gone?

Some think, for this reason, that Our Lord should have remained on earth. But Our Lord knew better. In answer to such a request, He said: "It is better for you that I should go away; he who is to befriend you, will not come to you unless I do go" (Jn 16:7). He is saying that if He remained on earth, we could never get any closer to Him than the touch of a hand, or the sound of a voice, or the thrill of an embrace, which is far below the degree of intimacy that God wants with the soul, and the soul desires with God. But if He ascended into heaven and sent to us His Spirit, then He would not be an example to be copied, but a veritable life to be lived. Then His mind would be our mind; His life, our life.

This much is *certain*. We who live nineteen hundred years after His birth should not be penalized for this accident of time and space. It may very well be that we have more need of Him now, than did the people of His time. I should be very much inclined to doubt His divinity, if He could not overcome the barriers of years and boundaries of space, and make the great gifts which He brought to Galilee and Judea available to London, New York, and Moscow; to the shepherds of Texas as well as Bethlehem, and to the fishermen of Massachusetts as well as Capharnaum.

If Christ is only the memory of someone who lived and suffered and died and who has left us orphans, then it is better to abandon Him. If Christianity is only the memory of some man who taught, governed, and sanctified hundreds of years ago, and then left us only a few records written by other men, then the sooner we forget it the quicker we can begin our search for the divine.

But Christ *does live.* He said that: "I shall be with you all days even to the consummation of the world." Our problem is to find out where and how He lives today. This is not hard. We begin with the fact that he first taught, governed, and sanctified *through* a human nature which was given to Him by His Mother who was overshadowed by the Holy Spirit. He *taught* through the body Mary gave Him; He governed through the body that Mary nursed; He sanctified through the body that Mary offered on the Cross for the redemption of the world.

This being so, I would not be at all surprised if that is not the way He will continue to live through the centuries, namely, in another body, this time not a physical and individual body like the one He took from Mary, but in a social and mysterious body such as He might take from the womb of humanity, and overshadow it with the same Holy Spirit. Thus as He taught, governed, and sanctified through His *physical* body, so He will continue to teach, govern, and sanctify through a social body which He would infuse with His Spirit and which He would govern as its head. If He ever sent His Spirit to it, then it would be a "mystical" body.

This desire to be one with Christ cannot be satisfied with sermons, books, and hymns. I can hear you say if He is only a memory, I do not want Him. I know what I do not want, and I know what I want. *I do not want* a dead truth spoken centuries ago. What is written in your books, in your Aristotles, and your Platos, can satisfy only for an hour. I want a living, breathing truth with a tongue. I want a power and authority over me that treats the subjects as sheep and lambs, and to whom no authority is given until three times he who is to enjoy it says to you, in the words of Peter: "O Christ, I love you, I love you, I love."

I want to be better in the sense of being sanctified, and I know that psychology cannot make me better because

I am only lifting myself with my own bootstraps. I want no sanctification that is just a warm feeling down in the pit of my stomach. I want forgiveness of my sins, *now*. I want Thy life, O Christ, in my body and in my blood: I want the living divine presence in me, so that I do not live, but rather Thou, O Christ, livest in me. I am human enough, too human; I want to be made a partaker of Thy divinity. This alone is sanctification.

If you asked me the three things we must have to be happy, I would say:

1. A wisdom beyond all the partial knowledge of earth.
2. A power greater than either man alone or man in society.
3. A love that would die if need be, to save us if we failed.

These three are in Christ, Who is infallible truth, divine power or authority, and heavenly love or holiness.

Now His truth is no more divine than Buddha's if it is available only in a few fragments written by men after His death; His power and authority is no more divine than Lincoln's if it is available only in a few biographies; and His love is no more heavenly than that of Socrates if we cannot have our sins forgiven now by Him, as did Magdalen and the penitent thief. Then if He did not prolong His truth, His authority, His holiness to us, then He is not good. If He could not, then He is not God.

But He is God, and He did provide to make His truth, authority, and life come to us in this later century. But how? In the same way He did then; through human nature. When you write, you use your hand as the visible and fleshy instrument of your invisible mind; so He, Who is God, in a more perfect way, taught, governed, and sanctified through His human nature, which was the visible instrument of His invisible divinity. In plain language, you would have seen His body; but you would have heard, obeyed, and been forgiven by God in Christ.

Our Lord said that He would take on a new body, and that through it He would continue to be united with us until the end of time. It would not be another physical body like that which he took from Mary. That human nature is now glorified at the right hand of His Father. He spoke of another kind of body. If you look up the word "body" in the dictionary, you will find it can mean one of two things: either something physical or something social, i.e., either our physical organism of flesh and blood which is vivified by a soul; or it can mean a social grouping of persons who are considered as a whole because they have the same ideals and help one another. For example, we speak of the nation as the "body politic", or of a group of university professors as an "educational body". This new body would not be like these, i.e., a *moral* body, for their unity comes from the will of men. Rather His new social body would be bound to Him not by the will of men, but by His heavenly Spirit, which He would send on leaving this earth.

Here are only seven of the many things He said about His social body which He would assume:

1. He told us that to be a member of His new body we would have to be born into it. But it would not be through a *human* birth, for that only makes us sons of Adam; to be a member of His new body we would have to be reborn through the Spirit in the waters of Baptism, which would make us sons of God.

2. The unity between this new body and Him would not be through singing hymns to him, or having social teas in His name, or listening to broadcasts,

but through sharing His Life: "I am the vine, you are its branches ... you have only to live on in me, and I will live on in you" (Jn 15:5).

3. His new body would be like all living things, small at first—even, as He said, "like a mustard seed", but it would grow from simplicity to complexity until the consummation of the world. As He put it: "first the blade, then the ear, then the perfect grain in the ear" (Mk 4:28, 29).

4. A house expands from the outside in, by the addition of brick to brick; human organizations grow by the addition of man to man, i.e., from the circumference to the center. His body, He said, would be formed from the inside out, as a living embryo is formed in the human body. As He received Life from the Father, we would receive life from Him. As He put it: "That they too may be one in us, as thou, Father, art in me, and I in Thee" (Jn 17:21).

5. Our Lord said that He would have only one body. It would be a spiritual monstrosity for Him to have many bodies, or a dozen heads. To keep it one, it would have one shepherd who, He said, would feed His lambs and His sheep. "There will be one fold, and one shepherd" (Jn 10:16).

6. He said that His new body would not manifest itself before men until the day of Pentecost when He would send His truth-giving Spirit. "He will not come to you unless I do go" (Jn 16:7). Anything that would start therefore, even twenty-four hours after Pentecost, or twenty-four hours ago would be an organization all right; it would have the human spirit, but it would not have the Holy Spirit; it would be like an electric wire that was not connected to a dynamo.

7. The most interesting observation He made about
   His body was that it would be hated by the world,
   as He was. Anything worldly, the world loves. But
   what is divine, the world hates. "Because I have sin-
   gled you out from the midst of the world, the world
   hates you" (Jn 15:19).

The nucleus of this new social body was to be His
Apostles. They were to be the raw material into which
He would send His Spirit to quicken them into His prolonged self. They would represent Him when He was
gone. The privilege of evangelizing the world was reserved
to them. This new body, of which they were the embryo,
was to be His posthumous self, and His prolonged personality, through the centuries.

Here we come to something really startling. Remember, Our Lord is teacher, King, and priest or Savior. But
now we find Him communicating to His new body His
triple office of teaching, governing, and sanctifying. He
Who is the infallible teacher and Who said: "I am the
Truth", now tells His body "I will send ... The truth-
giving Spirit, ... to guide you into all truth" (Jn 16:8, 13).
So much would He be identified with the new body,
that when anyone heard His body speak, they would
be hearing Him. "He who listens to you, listens to me; he
who despises you, despises me; and he who despises me,
despises him that sent me" (Lk 10:16). His truth would
be the new body's truth—and therefore infallible, divine,
heavenly truth.

Secondly, Our Lord Who is King, said: "All authority
in heaven and on earth has been given to me" (Mt 28:18).
This authority He so communicates to His body that its
commands are *His* commands; its orders are His orders,
which He ratifies. "I promise you, all that you bind on

earth shall be bound in heaven, and all that you loose on earth, shall be loosed in heaven" (Mt 18:18).

Finally, Our Lord is priest or mediator, for He redeemed us to God through His death on the Cross. This holiness and power of sanctification He now communicates to His new body. His new body is told to baptize, to offer the memorial of His death, and oh! what a blessed gift!—to forgive sins. "When you forgive men's sins, *they are forgiven*, when you hold them bound, they are held bound" (Jn 20:23).

The nucleus of this social body was the Apostles. But until Our Lord sent His Spirit on them fifty days after His Resurrection, they were like the elements in a chemical laboratory. We know up to 100% the chemicals which enter into the constitution of a human body, but we cannot make a baby because we lack the unifying principle of a soul. The Apostles could not give their body divine life any more than chemicals can make human life. They needed God's invisible, divine Spirit to unify their visible human natures.

Accordingly, ten days after the Ascension, the glorified Savior Who is in heaven sends upon them His Spirit, not in the form of a book, but as tongues of living fire. As cells in a body form a new human life when God breathes a soul into the embryo, so the Apostles appeared as the visible Body of Christ when the Holy Spirit came to make them one. This is called in tradition and Scripture the "whole Christ" or "the fullness of Christ".

The new body of Christ now appears publicly before men. Just as the Son of God took upon Himself a human nature from the womb of Mary, overshadowed by the Holy Spirit, so now He takes a new body from the womb of humanity, overshadowed by the Holy Spirit. Just as He once taught, governed, and sanctified through human nature, so now He continues to teach, to govern, and to sanctify through other human natures which make His body.

Because this body is not *physical* like a man, nor moral like a bridge club, but heavenly and spiritual because of the Spirit which made it one, it is called the Mystical Body. As my body is made up of millions and millions of cells, and yet is one because vivified by one soul, presided over by one visible head, and governed by an invisible mind, so this new body of Christ, though made up of millions and millions of persons who are incorporated into Christ by Baptism, is one because it is vivified by the Holy Spirit of God, and presided over by one visible head, and governed by one invisible mind or head Who is the risen Christ.

This Mystical Body is His prolonged self! That He is continuing to live in it now, recall the story of St. Paul whose Hebrew name was Saul. Perhaps no one ever lived who hated Christ more than Saul. The early members of Christ's Mystical Body prayed that God would send someone to refute him. God heard their prayer; He sent Paul to answer Paul. One day this persecutor, breathing with hatred, set out on a journey to Damascus to seize the members of Christ's Mystical Body there and bind them and bring them back to Jerusalem. The time was only a few years after the Ascension of Our Divine Savior. Remember that Our Lord is now glorified in heaven. Suddenly a great light shone about Saul and he fell to the ground. Aroused by a Voice like a bursting sea he hears: "Saul, Saul, why dost thou *persecute me?*" Nothingness dared to ask the name of omnipotence: "Who art thou, Lord?" And the Voice answered: "I am Jesus Whom Saul persecutes."

How could Saul be persecuting Our Lord Who is now glorified in heaven? Saul was doing nothing that Stalin did not do to Poland and Hungary. Why then should the

voice from heaven say: "Saul, Saul, why dost thou persecute me?"

Well, if someone stepped on your foot, would not your
head complain because it is part of your body? Our Lord is
now saying that in striking His body, Paul is striking Him.
When the body of Christ is persecuted, it is Christ the
invisible head Who arises to speak and to protest.

The Mystical Body of Christ therefore no more stands
between Christ and me, than His physical body stood between Magdalen and His forgiveness, or His hand stood
between the little children and His blessing. It was through
His human body that He came to men in His individual
Life; it is through His Mystical Body that He comes to us
in His mystical corporate life. Christ is living now! He is
teaching now, governing now, sanctifying now. He has
His glorious moments in other Palm Sundays; His scan-
dalous moments of history when other Judases betray;
and His suffering moments, as He has now in those like
Mindszenty who also "suffer under Pontius Pilate".

If you asked me what the body of Christ means to me, I
would say: "I believe that it is the temple of love, in which
I am a living stone, the cornerstone of which is Christ; it
is the tree of eternal life, of which I am a branch; it is the
body of Christ on earth since His Ascension into heaven,
and I am one of the cells of that body.

"The body of Christ is therefore more to me than I
am to myself; *her* Life—I shall call the body of Christ *her*
because the Bible calls it His spouse—her life is more
abundant than mine, for I live in union with her, and
without her I have only a physical life. Her loves are my
loves; her truths are my truths; her mind is my mind. I
consider that the greatest blessing Almighty God has given
to me is to be united with her. My greatest pain is not to
serve her better. Without her I am the uprooted stem, an

isolated column among dead and forgotten ruins. With her, I profess eternity and am not afraid. From her tabernacles I draw the Bread of Life, from her episcopal hands the oil that strengthens and blesses and consecrates; from her sanctuary lamp the assurance that Christ has not left us orphans."

Did you know that there were three men in history whose names were changed by God? But you do know *certainly* that a religion that started an hour ago is worthless— because it is man made. Even a religion that started nineteen hundred years ago is not necessarily divine. Really a divine religion ought to go back to the first moment when God created man. Then we would have God's idea of religion, not yours and mine.

If you study the history of revealed religion you discover two facts: (1) God extends His Mercies to mankind through a community of His choosing; (2) over this chosen body He divinely appoints a man as its head and His vicar.

In the very beginning of history God made the first man Adam as the head of mankind. As a father's crimes disgrace his family, so in a greater way Adam's sin became our sin. But God in His mercy promised a redeemer born of a woman who would crush the spirit of evil.

When sin multiplies on the face of the earth, God saves mankind in the flood, not by providing each man with an individual lifesaver. Rather, He selects a small community over which He divinely appoints one man—Noah. Through this little social body God promises blessings to the world.

Later on, God chooses another man, Abram, to be the head of a new race or religious body, and with him He enters into a new covenant. "In thee all the races of the world shall find a blessing" (Gen 12:3). It was the first time in history that God ever changed the name of a man. The true and almighty God changes his name from Abram to Abraham, which means "father of many nations". Through him, not only his own people, but the Gentiles are to be blessed. It is serious to take away a man's name, but obviously God did it to remind Abraham that his relation to the God-approved community was not personal, that is, his by right, but functional, that is, because of the role he fulfilled in it as God's vicar.

After the death of Abraham, the headship of the new spiritual organism passed on to the divinely chosen Isaac. Next came Jacob, who one night just before the dawn underwent a spiritual conflict "as fierce as the battling of men"; it was known as the wrestling with an angel. As Abraham's faith revealed God's spiritual strength, Jacob's triumph revealed man's spiritual strength. For the second time in history God changes the name of a man. He gives new and added power to the spiritual corporation or body which is destined to enrich the world through the coming of its savior, as God says to Jacob: "Thou shalt not be called Jacob any longer; *Israel* is to be thy name" (Gen 35:10).

Later, Moses was appointed by God as the head of the new chosen body, as God said: "I will make you *my* own people and will be your God" (Ex 6:7). "My own people." How the Egyptians must have accused the Jews of narrowness and intolerance for saying that God had made them the instrument through which His blessings would pass to all the world. But after all, since we are interested in God's ways, not man's, so be it. Evidently God has not given to each an individual planet; there is only one sun to light a world.

After Moses, there is Joshua, and later David, and the kings and the prophets. God never communicated His blessings to an individual for himself alone, nor to the world in general. He did it always through a corporate body with whom He entered into a covenant and over which He chose a head. Faithful or unfaithful, virtuous or sinful, infallible was the destiny of this religious Body. God was to be with this instrument He had chosen. No matter what it did, even though it fell among idolaters, even though some of the appointed heads were sinful, even though their love of the flesh damaged their efficiency, God's purposes went on and prevailed, for as it has been said: "God alone can write straight with crooked lines."

You can readily see that the most important word in the Old Testament was the word for this religious body of chosen people with its divinely appointed head, through which God would come to redeem man from sin. The Hebrew word for this elect body, or the divinely chosen community, was *qahal*.

About two hundred years before Christ was born, so many Jews were scattered throughout a Grecian civilization that it became necessary to translate the Hebrew Scriptures into Greek. This translation has since been called the Septuagint, because it was said to be done by seventy men. When they came across the word *qahal*, which stood for the community which was visible in its members, and yet invisible in the Spirit of God that watched and protected it, these learned old men translated this important Hebrew word *qahal*, which appears ninety-six times in the Old Testament, into the Greek word *ecclesia*.

Finally, in the fullness of time, He Whom the prophet foretold would be born in Bethlehem, and Who would be conceived by a virgin, now appears as God in the form of man: Our Lord and Savior, Jesus Christ. He is born in the *qahal* or *ecclesia* of the Jewish people. That is what the Gospel means when it tells us He came "into His own".

But, and this is important, He also said that He came not to destroy His *qahal* or *ecclesia*, but to fulfill it and perfect it. But before He would do this men would have to know Who He is, for He hit history with such an impact He split it in two.

The scene took place in the half-pagan city of Caesarea Philippi. He, the Lord and Master of the world, stopped to ask a question—the most important one He ever asked in His life: "What do *men* say of the Son of Man? Who do they think He is?" (Mt 16:13). Notice: "What do *men* say?" It was a test for religion based on the majority idea, the poll, public opinion, or the individual's interpretation of his own emotional experiences. "What do *men* say?" The answer was one of total confusion. "Some say John the Baptist," they told Him, "others Elijah, others again Jeremiah, or one of the prophets" (Mt 16:14). All rudimentary guesses of the poor and ignorant! No certainty! No agreement! No unity so dear to the heart of God! Leave the secret of His divinity to polls, to masses and majority votes, and you get only contradictory, contrary, and confusing responses, one man denying what another has said! Our Lord had for this confusion only the withering scorn of His silence.

Our Lord now turns from quantity to quality, from the mob to the intelligentsia. He questions the senate, the federation, the parliament, the House of Lords, as He says to them: "And what of you? Who do you say that I am?" (Mt 16:15). You, my council, my followers! Not men, but *you.* . . . And the twelve Apostles do not answer. Why are they silent? Because, perhaps, if they all spoke at once there would be only confusion of tongues; because, if one spoke for the others too, they would have asked who gave him authority to speak; because they knew down deep in their hearts that if the answer was to be based on the majority, then God's truth would not be absolute.

There was no certitude in the conciliar body any more than among the individuals. Men will never agree among themselves; the best they can do is to federate their guesses. Such federations of opinions are like spiritual archipelagoes, little islands separated from one another by whirling waters of scepticism, and united only in fiction by a common name. There is no one to speak for them; there is no authority; there is no *head*; there is therefore no unity. A body without a head is a monstrosity whether the body be physical, social, or religious.

Something now happens which is less of man than of God. One man now steps forward. It is he who is always mentioned first in every list of the Apostles.

He is named 195 times in the Gospels, while all the other Apostles together are mentioned only 130 times. He is the only person, outside of His heavenly Father, whom Our Lord so united to Himself as to say "We". He is also the third man in history whose name is changed by God. We may suspect then that as with Abraham and in Jacob, some new and unheard of perfection is to be given to the *qahal* or *ecclesia*. This man's original name was Simon, son of Jonah. When Our Lord first saw him, a year and a half before this scene, He said: "Thou art Simon, the son of Jonah"; then Our Lord changed his name: "Thou shalt be called Cephas (which means rock)." He changes his name from Simon to Rock. We do not have the full flavor of this in English because Peter, the name of a man, is different from the word Rock. But in the original Aramaic, which Our Lord spoke, Cephas, which is his new name, means Rock. It is something like the French where the word *pierre* is not only the name of a man but also means *rock*.

This same man whose name was changed to Rock now steps forward, not because the Apostles asked him to do so, not because he was smarter than the others, or because he knew the answer in his own flesh and blood, but because there came to him a great light, a light that made him first for eternity. That heavenly revelation gave him the answer to the question of the Master as with infallible certitude he affirms: "Thou art the Christ, the Son of the living God" (Mt 16:16).

Peter knew Who He was. He was not John the Baptist! He was not Elijah! He was the One for Whom the Gentile and Jewish world had been expectantly looking for so many centuries. He is Emmanuel! God with us! The Son of the living God! Jesus Christ, true God and true man! The moment he said it he was certain he had divine assistance. And Our Lord told him that was how he knew it as He said: "Blessed art thou, Simon, son of Jonah; it is not flesh and blood, it is my Father in heaven that has revealed this to thee" (Mt 16:17).

At this moment Simon, the descendant of Abraham, who revealed the power of God, and the descendant of Jacob, who revealed the power of man, combines in himself the powerful initiative of a human will cooperating with the infallible assistance of a heavenly Father, the God-man who changed his name now sets him at the head of the new and perfected religious body, a new Israel, a new Christ-qahal, a divine ecclesia with these words: "And I tell thee this in my turn, that thou art Peter, and it is upon this rock that I will build my Ecclesia, and the gates of hell shall not prevail against it; and I will give to thee the keys of the kingdom of heaven; and whatever thou shalt bind on earth shall be bound in heaven, and whatever thou shalt loose on earth shall be loosed in heaven" (Mt 16:17–19).

Our Divine Lord leaves nothing undetermined about his new qahal or ecclesia, for he spoke of three things: its foundation, what is outside it, and what is inside it, and all

three revolved about one man. The *foundation* is the Rock
who is Peter; the door to the *ecclesia* from the outside is to
be opened by keys, and these keys swing from the cincture
of Peter; once on the inside the same rock and key-bearer
has the power to bind and loose, to seal and unseal consciences even for registry in the book of life.

Now the time has come to translate the word *qahal* or
ecclesia into English. It means "church", and so Our Lord
meant it when He said: "Thou art Peter, and it is upon this
rock, that I will build My Church."

What would you say is the major peril in the world
today? I would say it is authoritarianism, for it includes
not only communism, but all those old and new forms of
state supremacy and political dictatorship which destroy
freedom.

Authoritarianism enslaves in three ways: (1) by subject-
ing the mind to dogmas and systems; (2) by making fear the
basis of authority; (3) by destroying freedom of thought.

Our Divine Savior lived and grew up under an authoritarian system which tyrannized His people. When, therefore, He began prolonging His Life to His Mystical Body
the Church, He made it a bulwark against all forms of
authoritarianism, contrasting the two in these words: "You
know that among the Gentiles those who bear rule, lord
it over them, and great men vaunt their power over them;
with you it must be otherwise; . . . and whoever has a mind
to be first among you must be your slave" (Mt 20:25–27).

How thankful we should be to Our Dear Lord for saving us as members of His Mystical Body from the terrible menace of authoritarianism. He does it in three ways:
(1) because in the Church we obey not a system, but a person; (2) because in the Church the basis of our obedience
is not fear but love; and (3) because in the Church our

freedom of thought is saved from narrowness by knowing both sides of a question.

1. In authoritarianism one must submit to a system, that is, to a complicated network of dogmas and assumptions, superstitions and codes, directives and orders which are always abstract and impersonal, such as, dialectical materialism, or class conflict, or the labor theory of value. But as Catholics we do not subscribe to a system of dogmas; we began with a person, namely, the person of Jesus Christ continued in His Mystical Body. Our faith is the meeting of two personalities: Our Lord and you. There is no adhesion to an abstract dogma, but rather communion with a person who can neither deceive nor be deceived. The authoritarian starts with a party line; we start with Our Divine Lord, the Son of the living God Who said: "I am the truth." Truth therefore is personal. As the love of a child for its home is more than the sum of the commands of its parents, so our love for the Church is more than the sum of the truths which express that faith. Our faith is first and foremost in Christ, living in His Mystical Body, and then only secondly in explicit beliefs. If He did not reveal them, we would not believe them. If we lost Him, we would lose our beliefs. He comes first; everything else is secondary.

There is no doctrine, no moral, no dogma, no liturgy, no belief apart from Him. *He* is the object of our faith, and not a dogma. As the dogma that a young man should give a ring to the young lady to whom he is engaged is secondary to his love of her as a person, so nothing to us is credible apart from Christ in His Mystical Body. If we believed that Our Lord were not God, but only a good man who lived 1900 years ago, we would never believe in the Eucharist, or the Trinity. If we believed that all Our Lord left was a few shorthand notes transcribed by secretaries some years after His death, we would not believe in the forgiveness of sins. But because we know that Our Lord once taught, governed, and sanctified through a body taken from the womb of His Mother overshadowed by the Holy Spirit, and is now living, teaching, and governing today in His Mystical Body taken from the womb of humanity and overshadowed by the same Holy Spirit, we accept every single word of His, not only what His secretaries wrote but also His memory or tradition through these nineteen hundred years. We want no institution standing between Our Lord and us. And His Mystical Body no more stands between Him and us than my body stands between me and my visible head or between me and my invisible mind. His Mystical Body the Church is what St. Augustine fifteen hundred years ago, called the *Totus Christus*, the *Whole Christ*. Thank God for your faith in the person of the living Christ, the eternal contemporary. It is the hope of the world against authoritarianism.

2. The Church, the Mystical Body of Christ, saves us from authoritarianism with its police systems and propaganda because the basis of our faith is not fear, but love. Because authoritarianism is based on a system, it begets fear. Because we start with the person of Christ in His Mystical Body, we believe not through fear, but with love. One cannot love dialectical materialism or ethical cosmopolitanism, nor pragmatic humanism, but one can love a person. Between our created personality and His uncreated personality there is a bond of love. So inseparable are the two that Our Lord did not communicate to Peter the power of ruling and governing His Church until three times Peter had told Our Lord that he loved Him above all else.

The submission we make to Our Savior in His Mystical Body is something like the loving submission that we make to the best and oldest and wisest of our friends, or the obedience a son gives to his father. We feel no distance between us who are taught, and the Church of Christ which teaches. As a pupil more and more absorbs the teachings of the professor, the less becomes the distance between them. There finally comes a moment when there is a partnership begotten of love for that common truth. The more we know Our Lord and obey the truth manifested through His Body, the Church, the less we feel under Him. The more His truth becomes ours, the more we love Him. To fall from faith in Our Lord in His Mystical Body is like falling from friendship with a person we love, to the abstract love of a book which he wrote, or a trinket which he wore. I cannot imagine anything more cold, more enslaving, more paralyzing to human reason, more destructive of freedom than that thing to which millions are prostrating every day, the terrible anonymous authority of "they". "They say." "They are wearing navy blue this year." "They say that Catholics adore Mary." "They say that hair will be shorter this year." "They say that Freud is the thing." Who are *they*? Countless slaves and puppets are bowing down daily before that invisible, tyrannical myth of "they". No wonder dictators arose to personalize that terrible slavery!

But we *know* in whom we believe: Our Lord living in His Mystical Body.

3. The Church, the Mystical Body of Christ, saves us from authoritarianism because it gives us not freedom *from* thought, but freedom of thought. The devil has pretty well convinced some of his subjects that they should not accept the authority of Christ, because they would be weakening their reason. He suggests that any limitation put upon reason is due to a sinister cause. In the Garden he suggested

that not to know evil, whether it be of the mind such as communism, or of the body such as cancer, is to destroy freedom. So the devil told our first parents, "The purpose of God is to prevent free inquiry. He wants to keep the human race in ignorance. Do not be fooled. He is an old 'fuddy-duddy' and reactionary. Be liberal." God is thus made to appear as an enemy of truth and free inquiry, in the same way that a father who refuses to let his five-year-old son have a shotgun, is said by some to be denying the freedom of the son.

The error of the devil is that continuance in loyalty and love means discontinuance in mental growth. To the devil, to continue to be loyal to the wife, a country, an ideal, is a mark of slavery and a want of freedom.

There is, however, *one* sense in which the Church restricts reason and that is in the same way that all truth restricts it. Before I went to school I was free to believe that Shakespeare was born in 1224, but after a little education, I had to stop such liberalism and freedom of thought. I was also free to believe that H_2O were the initials of a spy, but the school soon became "reactionary" and put a stop to that kind of thinking by telling me it was the symbol for water.

Freedom is not in liberation *from* truth, but in the acceptance of truth. I am free to draw a triangle only on condition that I accept the truth of the triangle, and give it three sides, and not in a stroke of broadmindedness give it thirty-three sides. This is what Our Lord meant when He said: "The truth will set you free" (Jn 8:32).

5

Christian Life Is Struggle

There is a law written across the universe that no one shall be crowned unless he has first struggled. No halo of merit rests suspended over those who do not fight. Icebergs that float in the cold streams of the north do not command our respectful attention just for being icebergs; but if they were to float in the warm waters of the Gulf Stream without dissolving, they would command awe and wonderment. They might, if they did it on purpose, be said to have character.

The only way one can ever prove love is by making an act of choice; mere words are not enough. Hence, the original trial given to man has been given again to all men; even the angels have passed through a trial. Ice deserves no credit for being cold, nor fire for being hot; it is only those who have the possibility of choice that can be praised for their acts. It is through temptation and its strain that the depths of character are revealed. Scripture says: "Blessed is he who endures under trials. When he has proved his worth, he will win that crown of life, which God has promised to those who love him" (Jas 1:12). The defenses of the soul are seen at their strongest when the evil which has been resisted is also strong. The presence of temptation does not necessarily imply moral imperfection on the part of the one who is tempted. In that case, Our Divine Lord could not have been tempted at all. An inward tendency toward evil, such as man has, is not a necessary condition for an onslaught of temptation. The temptation of Our Blessed Lord came only from without, and not from within as ours so often does. What was at stake in the trial of Our Lord was not the perversion of natural appetites to which the rest of men are tempted; rather, it was an appeal to Our Lord to disregard His divine mission and His Messianic work. The temptation that comes from without does not necessarily weaken character; indeed, when conquered, it affords an opportunity for holiness to increase.

The temptations of man are easy enough to analyze, because they always fall into one of three categories: they pertain to the flesh (lust and gluttony), or to the mind (pride and envy), or to the idolatrous love of things (greed). Though man is buffeted all through life by these three kinds of temptation, they vary in intensity from age to age. It is during youth that man is most often tempted against purity and inclined to the sins of the flesh; in middle age, the flesh is less urgent and temptations of the mind begin to predominate, e.g., pride and the lust for power; in the autumn of life, temptations to avarice are likely to assert themselves. Seeing that the end of life is near, man strives to banish doubts about eternal security or salvation, by piling up the goods of earth and redoubling his economic security. It is a common psychological experience that those who have given way to lust in youth are often those who sin by avarice in their old age.

Good men are not tempted in the same way as evil men, and the Son of God, Who became man, was not tempted in the same way as even a good man. The temptations of an alcoholic to "return to his vomit", as Scripture puts it, are not the same as the temptations of a saint to pride, though they are, of course, no less real.

Because we have tendencies to evil there must be self-denial or the pulling out of the weeds, in order that the divine life of grace may grow.

Nature itself suggests mortification. In addition to the anabolic, or binding up of life, there is yet another process of life, viz: the catabolic, which corresponds to contraction in the mineral order. Iron not only expands when it is heated, but it also contracts when it is cooled. Life not only nourishes itself but becomes the nourishment for other kinds of life. The various orders of creation are so many different expressions of this law. The plant not only consumes the hydrogen, oxygen, sunlight, and water which are necessary for its life, but in its turn becomes food for the animal; the animal not only nourishes itself on the plants of the field, but even gives its life for man in order to be served as food at his table. Once a thing has been nourished by a kingdom below, it becomes, in its turn, the nourishment of a kingdom above it. If this law did not exist all life would perish from the earth. If the chemical kingdom in a selfish way would refuse to give itself to plants, if the sky would refuse to bless the plant with its rain, all plant life would perish from the earth. If the plant in a selfish way would refuse to give its nourishment to the animal in the field; if the seed would refuse to give itself as food to the bird; if the sea would refuse to feed the fish—then all animal life would pass away from this earth. If the chemicals and the plants and the animals would refuse to give their energies and their lives for man, then all human life would pass away from this earth. In other words, life must not only expand by growing, but must die by contraction in order to become the food of a higher life. The whole universe would be a world of parasites if things did not give up their lives for other things.

What are the benefits of immolation? First, is it just that life should exist for other life? We can answer this question by asking another. Has the plant life within itself? Has the animal a perfect life? Does not the very fact that plants and animals and man need nourishment prove that they have not a perfect life, but that they are dependent on other life? Only God has perfect life. If nothing has perfect life but God, shall we deny to this imperfect life the right to live? And if we admit the right to live, we admit the right to live on a lower plane of life. Shall we deny reciprocity in the order of living things? Is it not just that if things nourish themselves on others, they in turn should become the nourishment of something higher? In other words, it is only just that if things consume, they shall also be consumed; if they immolate, they shall also be immolated; if they receive, they shall also give.

What is the benefit and the purpose of all this? What high purpose could God have had in imposing this law of immolation on the actual universe? He has a most wonderful plan if we would but study it closely, and His plan is to give to each of the kingdoms a higher life than they naturally possess. The mineral kingdom, the air, the sunlight, the carbonates and the like have no life. But what happens to them once they enter into the plant? The plant does not destroy them; it does not blot out their existence; it takes away nothing either from their dignity or their role, but it adds something to them. It ennobles the mineral by associating it with its life; it makes it share a life which it never enjoyed before. It gives the mineral new laws; it confers on it the dignity of plant life. In other words, it elevates the nature of the mineral kingdom.

The same benefit accrues to the animal kingdom. As the mineral gives itself up in order to live a higher life in the plant, so too does the plant immolate itself for the animal in order to have its life ennobled in the animal. The plant is torn up from the soil by the roots; it is plucked from the pasture by the devouring teeth of beasts; it is ground as food and passes into the animal organism. But in passing into the animal it does not cease to be plant life; if it did it would never nourish the animal. What does happen is that it now begins to be governed by other laws directed to new purposes, organized in new cells—in a word, the plant now begins to take on a higher life.

But is there anything which can ennoble the existence of man? Is there anyone for whom man can die to himself in order that he might have a higher kind of existence? If there were not, what a terrible world this would be! We have no right to say there is no higher life than man, any more than the rose has a right to say there is no higher life than itself. Suppose the order of the universe stopped with man. Then the plant would be higher than man for the plant could continue its existence in an ennobled way in the animal; then the animal would be higher than man for the animal could have its existence enriched in man. Certainly there must be some nature above the nature of man into which man can be assumed in order that he might be supernaturalized. There must be some higher kind of life which will be the perfection of human life in a way immeasurably superior to the perfection of plant life in an animal. And what is this life?

It is the life of God, a life infinitely distant and remote from the life of man. We have seen the different processes by which the lower creation shares in the life of the higher. But when we consider that mystery, "hidden in God from all eternity", the elevation of man to be a "sharer of the divine nature", there exists nothing in creation resembling it. We may see some faint analogy in the examples already given, but they are the examples of created things. From

the life of God, every creature—even the highest angel—
must be forever excluded. Yet God has communicated this
life, freely and gratuitously, to intellectual creatures. God
could have done this wondrous thing in various possible
ways, but He has revealed to us the way He has chosen.
God Himself designed to become a sharer in our humanity
in order that we might share in His divinity. Christ Our
Lord is the link between us and God. Because He has a
human nature He is like unto us in all things save sin;
because He has a divine nature in the unity of person, He
is God. The common denominator between Him and us is
His human nature. This is the link between us and the life
of God.

Now if we are to live the higher life, if we are to become
incorporated into the life of God, if we are to have our life
ennobled, then we must in some way enter into the life of
Christ. We must become one with Him if we are to share
in His life.

What is the inspiration of this law of dying to ourselves
in order to live to another? What mysterious energy is it
that inspired the Incarnate Word to make our dead selves
stepping stones to higher things? It is love. Love is the
inspiration of all sacrifice. And love, be it understood, is
not the desire to have, to own, to possess—that is selfishness. Love is the desire *to be had, to be owned; to be possessed.* It is the giving of oneself for another. The symbol
of love as the world understands it is the circle continually
surrounded by self, thinking only of self. The symbol of
love as Christ understands it, is the cross with its arms outstretched even unto eternity to embrace all souls within its
grasp. Sinful love as the world understands it finds its type
in Judas the night of the betrayal: "What will you give me
and I will deliver Him unto you." Love, in its true sense,
finds its type in Christ a few hours later when, mindful of

his disciples, he says to the friends of the traitor who blistered His lips with a kiss, "If therefore you seek Me, let these go their way."

Love then is the giving of self and as long as we have a body and are working out our salvation, it will always be synonymous with sacrifice, in the Christian sense of the word. Love sacrifices naturally just as the eye sees and the ear hears. That is why we speak of "arrows" and "darts" of love—something that wounds. The bridegroom who loves will not give his bride a ring of tin or of brass, but one of gold or of platinum, because the gold or platinum ring represents sacrifice—it *costs* something. The mother who sits up all night nursing her sick child does not call it hardship, but love. The day men forget that love is synonymous with sacrifice, that day they will ask what selfish sort of woman it must have been who ruthlessly extracted tribute in the form of flowers, or what an avaricious creature she must have been who demanded solid gold in the form of a ring, just as they will ask what cruel kind of God is it who asks for sacrifice and self-denial. And if there is a young lover in the world who will do anything for the one he loves, then I do not find it unreasonable that a God should so love the world as to send into it His only-begotten Son. And if a father will lay down his life for his son then I shall not find it unreasonable that the Son of God should lay down His life for His friends, "for greater love than this no man hath."

Such an analogy is imperfect, for Our Lord did more than follow a mere law of nature. His love was so great, His condescension and sacrifice so great, that any attempt to make them reasonable according to the dictates of human reason must always fall short of the truth. If all lovers tend to become like those they love, then I shall not be surprised to find creatures who will lay down their lives for their divine lover; and who will become so much like Him that they will carry about on their body the stigmata of the Passion. Love is the reason of all immolation. So too the man who loves his perfected life in Christ will die to himself, and this dying to himself, this taming of his members as so many wild beasts, this being imprinted with the cross, is mortification. Christ then gave no new law when He said that we must fall to the ground and, like a seed, die. He merely restated a law which our experience has verified a thousand times and still has not yet learned to apply to every corner of the universe, and particularly those corners of our souls which need it so badly.

Love, simply because it does inspire mortification, is foolishness from the world's point of view. No one ever quite understands the lovers but the lovers themselves; they live in a universe apart; they breathe another atmosphere; they do the unexpected, the unreal, the irrational—even the foolish. It is the law of love. Love implies sacrifice and sacrifice seems foolish to the world.

If love is equivalent to sacrifice and all sacrifice from the world's point of view is foolishness, Christ on the Cross is the supreme folly. From the standpoint of the world He was the greatest failure in history; in the ledger of the world's estimate of things, He suffered the greatest defeat. First of all, He could not win and could not keep friends. Peter, His chief apostle, denied Him to a maidservant; John, who leaned on His breast, was silent when the Master was accused; Judas, whom he had called to be one of the judges of the twelve tribes of Israel, sold Him for thirty pieces of silver. In His four trials, before the four judges, He failed to have a single witness to testify in His favor. He could not keep His friends, and is not that the test of one's success in life?

More than that, if He were God, why did He not try to win the favor of Pilate when he said, "Know you not that I have power to release you?" He could have won His freedom by ingratiating Himself with the Roman governor, and He did not.

"Folly", cries the world.

If He is all powerful, why does He not strike dead those who scourge and mock Him?

"Folly", again cries the world.

If He could raise up children of Abraham from the stones, why could He not raise up friends at the moment of arrest?

"Folly", cries the world.

If He could have won His release from Herod with just a miracle, why did He not work one?

"Folly", cries the world.

If He could sustain the whole world in the palm of His hand, why did He permit Himself to fall beneath the weight of the cross?

"Folly", cries the world.

If the magic touch of His hands could restore sight to the blind and hearing to the deaf, why did He permit hard nails to pierce them?

"Folly", cries the world.

If He could have proven His divinity by coming down from the cross, "Let Him now come down from the cross and we will believe Him", why did He not step down as a king from his throne?

"Folly", cries the world.

As a demagogue He would have succeeded; as a God He was crucified. The Cross is a folly and Christ a failure. So says the world.

Hence it is that every lover of Christ and Him crucified must share His folly. The law is no different for the disciple than for the Master. The world calls everyone a fool who leaves his riches and his friends, his wine and his song, for the cloister or the convent, and exchanges his silks and

satins for the hair shirt and the discipline. The world calls
him a fool who does not strike back when he is struck
and who does not malign when he is maligned; for is it
not divine foolishness to say: "To him that striketh thee
on the one cheek, offer also the other"? The world calls
him a fool who follows the so-called old and "antiquated"
laws of the Church on the sanctity of marriage and rejects
the modern views that glorify license and lust. The world
brands him as a fool who hangs himself on the cross of
mortification when he might come down and shake dice
with the soldier even for the garments of a God.

Yes, but "the foolishness of God is wiser than men",
and "the wisdom of this world is foolishness with God." It
is only from the world's point of view that we are a fool,
as our Master was before the court of Herod. In the sublime words of St. Paul, "We are fools for Christ's sake."
Common sense never drove any man mad; common sense
is said to be sanity and yet common sense never scaled
mountains and much less has it ever cast them into the sea.
Common sense is not violence and yet, "the kingdom of
heaven suffereth violence, and the violent bear it away."
Common sense never makes a man lose his life, and yet it
is in losing our life that we shall save it. Life sometimes can
be saved by stepping within an inch of death in jumping
a precipice, but common sense never makes the leap. The
soldier at times can cut his way out from his enemies but
he must have a carelessness about dying—and common
sense has not that carelessness. The Kingdom of heaven
can sometimes be gained only by plucking out an eye—
but common sense never plucked it out. "It is common
sense that makes a man die for the sake of dying", it is
love which makes a man die for the sake of living—and
so too, it is this love of Jesus Christ and Him crucified,
which produces the wisdom of heaven at the cost of the

foolishness of earth; which makes men throw down their lives to take them up again; which makes men sell fields for the pearl of great price; which makes men fling "the world a trinket at their wrist", laugh at death, and say with a modern saint, "I need no resignation to die but resignation to live." This does not mean the Gospel of Christ is a gospel of sorrow.

Consider the words of Cardinal Newman: "It is but a superficial view of things to say that this life is made for pleasure and happiness. To those who look under the surface, it tells a very different tale. The doctrine of the Cross does but teach, though infinitely more forcibly, still after all it does but teach the very same lesson which this world teaches to those who live long in it, who have much experience in it, who know it. The world is sweet to the lips, but bitter to the taste. It pleases us at first, but not at last. It looks gay on the outside, but evil and misery lie concealed within. When a man has passed a certain number of years in it, he cries out with the Preacher, 'Vanity of vanities, all is vanity.' Nay, if he has not religion for his guide, he will be forced to go further, and say: 'All is vanity and vexation of spirit'; all is disappointment; all is sorrow; all is pain. The sore judgments of God upon sin are concealed within it, and force a man to grieve whether he will or no. Therefore the doctrine of the Cross of Christ does but anticipate for us the experience of the world.... The Gospel ... hinders us from taking a superficial view, and finding a vain transitory joy in what we see; but it forbids our immediate enjoyment, only to grant enjoyment in truth and fullness afterwards. It only forbids us to *begin* with enjoyment. It only says, if you begin with pleasure you will end in pain. It bids us begin with the Cross of Christ, and in that Cross we shall at first find sorrow, but in a while peace and comfort will rise out of that sorrow.

That Cross will lead us to mourning, repentance, humiliation, prayer, fasting; we shall sorrow for our sins, we shall sorrow with Christ's suffering; but all this sorrow will only issue, nay, will be undergone in a happiness far greater than the enjoyment which the world gives—though careless worldly minds indeed will not believe this, ridicule the notion of it, because they never have tasted it, and consider it a mere matter of words, which religious persons think it decent and proper to use, and try to believe themselves, and get others to believe, but which no one really feels.... They alone are able truly to enjoy this world who begin with the world unseen. They alone enjoy it, who have first abstained from it. They alone can truly feast, who have first fasted; they alone are able to use the world, who have learned not to abuse it; they alone inherit it, who take it as a shadow of the world to come, and who for that world to come relinquish it."[1]

The purpose of self-discipline is, thus, not to destroy freedom but to perfect it. Freedom does not mean our right to do whatever we like, but to do whatever we ought; a man does not become free as he becomes licentious, but as he diminishes the traces of original sin. Self-denial is a denuding of the ego—it seeks to make the I free to follow God. The more the ego knocks off the chains which bind it to things outside itself, the freer it is to be its own, its *I*. As the drunkard is liquor-possessed, so the saint is self-possessed. There is a potential nobility or even divinity in all of us, as there is a potential statue in a crude block of marble. But before the marble can ever reveal the image, it must be subjected to the disciplinary actions of a chisel in the hands of a wise and loving artist, who knocks

[1] John Henry Newman, *Parochial and Plain Sermons*, bk. 6, no. 7 (San Francisco: Ignatius Press, 1977), 1241–45.

off huge chunks of formless egotism until the new and beautiful image of Christ Himself appears.

Self-discipline, then, is not an end in itself but a means to an end. Those who make self-discipline the essence of religion reject some of God's creatures as evil; generally they become proud. But detachment, properly practiced, is only a means of attachment to God. When there is no love of Him, there is no true self-discipline. St. Paul tells us that philanthropy, sacrifice, alms, even martyrdom, if embraced for any reason except love of God does not deserve an eternal reward. "I may give away all that I have, to feed the poor; I may give myself up to be burnt at the stake; if I lack charity, it goes for nothing" (1 Cor 13:3).

In the romantic order, a youth reveals his love for a girl by a surrender of other women's friendships and a concentration on the beloved. In the spiritual order, the soul reveals its love of God by a detachment from creatures and an attachment to the Creator alone.

The past stays with us in our habits, in our consciousness of remembered guilt, in our proclivity to repeat the same sin. Our past experiences are in our blood, our brains, and even in the very expression that we wear. The future judgment is also with us; it haunts us, causing our anxieties and fears, our dreads and preoccupations, giving us insecurity and uncertainty. A cow or a horse lives for the present moment, without remorse or anxiety; but man not only drags his past with him, but he is also burdened with worries about his eternal future.

Because the past is with him in the form of remorse or guilt, because the future is with him in his anxiety, it follows that the only way man can escape either burden is by reparation—making up for the wrong done in the past—and by a firm resolution to avoid such sin in the future. Disposing of the past is the first step to take, and in taking it, the important distinction between forgiveness and reparation for sin should be remembered. Some who have done wrong mistakenly think that they should only forget it, now that it is past and "done with"; others believe, falsely, that once a wrong deed has been forgiven, nothing further need be done. But both of these attitudes are incomplete, lacking in love. As soon as a soul comes in contact with Our Lord and realizes it has wounded such love, its first response after being forgiven is apt to be that of Zachary: "I will repay all." Our Lord, in instituting the Sacrament of Penance, made it clear that there is a difference between forgiveness and the undoing of the past. That is why confession is followed by absolution, or forgiveness, and why, when absolution has been given, the confessor says: "For your penance...." Then he tells the penitent what prayers to say or which good actions to perform to make atonement for his sins.

The high reasonableness of this is apparent if we translate the offense against God into purely human terms. Suppose that I have stolen your watch. When my conscience finally pricks me, I admit it all to you and say: "Will you forgive me?" No doubt you will, but I am sure that you will also say: "Give me back the watch." Returning the watch is the best proof of the sincerity of my regret. Even children know there must be a restoration of the balance, or equilibrium, disturbed by sin: a boy who breaks a window playing ball often volunteers, "I'll pay for it." Forgiveness alone does not wipe out the offense. It is as if a man, after every sin, were told to drive a nail into a board and, every time he was forgiven, a nail were pulled out. He would soon discover that the board was full of holes which had not been there in the beginning. Similarly, we cannot go back to the innocence that our sins have destroyed.

When we turned our backs upon God by sinning against Him, we burned our bridges behind us; now they have to be rebuilt with patient labor. A businessman who has contracted heavy debts will find his credit cut off; until he has begun to settle the old obligations, he cannot carry on his business. Our old sins must be paid for before we can continue with the business of living.

Reparation is the act of paying for our sins. When *that* is done, God's pardon is available to us. His pardon means a restoration of the relationship of love—just as, if we offend a friend, we do not consider that we are forgiven until the friend loves us again. God's mercy is always present. His forgiveness is forever ready, but it does not become operative until we show Him that we really value it. The father of the Prodigal Son had forgiveness always waiting in his heart; but the Prodigal Son could not avail himself of it until he had such a change of disposition that he asked to be forgiven and offered to do penance as a servant in his father's house. So long as we continue our attachment to evil, forgiveness is impossible; it is as simple as the law which says that living in the deep recesses of a cave makes sunlight unavailable to us. Pardon is not automatic—to receive it, we have to make ourselves pardonable. The proof of our sorrow over having offended is our readiness to root out the vice that caused the offense. The man who holds a violent grudge against his neighbor and who confesses it in the Sacrament of Penance cannot be forgiven unless he forgives his enemy. "If you do not forgive, your Father Who is in heaven will not forgive your transgressions either" (Mk 11:26).

At the root of much disorder is self-love, the error in living which hatches out a brood of seven major effects of egotism. These—the seven pallbearers of character—are pride, avarice, envy, lust, anger, gluttony, sloth. It is against these seven major forms of egotism that self-knowledge is directed.

Pride is too great admiration of oneself. The ultimate stage of pride is to make oneself his own law, his own judge, his own morality, his own god.

In the modern world, pride disguises itself under the prettier names of success and popularity. The modern man's desire to serve the best liquor, his woman's ambition to be the best dressed, the college sophomore's hope of being the most studiously unkempt—these are symptoms of an egotistical vanity which makes its owners dread not being noticed. Criticism, backbiting, slander, barbed words, and character assassination are acts of egotism intent on elevating the ego on the carcass of another's reputation; each depression of another's ego is made an elevation of one's own. The more important the egotist feels himself to be, the more irritated he becomes when he does not receive worship; those who flatter him are called wise— those who criticize him are condemned as fools.

Pride has seven evil fruits: *boasting*, or self-glorification through one's own words; *love of publicity*, which is conceit in what other people say; *hypocrisy*, which is pretending to be what one is not; *hardheadedness*, which is a refusal to believe that any other opinion is better than one's own; *discord*, or refusing to give up one's own will; *quarreling* whenever others challenge the wishes of the ego; and *disobedience*, or the refusal to submit one's ego to a lawful superior. Very often conceited people regard getting their own will as a more important gain than obtaining the thing which is withheld: it is the victory they value, not the spoils. That is why they will refuse to accept a gift that was not given to them at once when they first expressed their desire: they would rather punish the friend who did not instantly yield to them than have the object he withheld. In arguments they do not want to know the truth, but only to vindicate their own self-importance, to reaffirm their own opinions.

Avarice is a perversion of the natural right of every man to extend his personality by owning the things which minister to the needs of his body and his soul. Its disorder can come from desiring wealth as an *end* rather than as a means, or through the *manner* in which wealth is sought, with its disregard of others' rights, or in the way in which the money is *used*—to increase one's capital without limit, instead of using the excess to minister to the needs of others.

Avarice is a sign that one does not trust in God but feels the need to be his own providence. "So much for the man who would have none of God's help, but relied on his store of riches, and found his strength in knavery!" (Ps 52:7 [51:8–9]). Unless corrected, avarice leads to several other serious defects of character: it causes an insensibility to the suffering and the needs of others; it creates anxiety and restlessness in the soul, which is continually bent on the pursuit of "more"; it leads to violence against others in the cause of protecting wealth; to lying, that the owner may acquire more; to perjury, that he may protect his hoard; and to treachery, as in the case of Judas.

Excessive love of luxury and ease is another sign of nakedness of the soul. The less character a person has, the more he needs to supplement it by external show: furs, diamonds, jewels, yachts are so many vain attempts to make the poverty-stricken ego rich. *Having* is confused with *being*; the egotist imagines that *he* is worth more, merely because he owns something that has worth. This is the one sin which is most apt to provoke contempt when we see it in others, and pride when we practice it ourselves. It is a psychological fact that the avaricious man who disguises himself as "devoted to business" is extremely difficult to spiritualize. He lives under the illusion that he needs nothing, because the only needs he admits are those which supply the body. "And Jesus looked around, and said to His disciples, 'With what difficulty will those who have riches enter God's Kingdom'" (Mk 10:23).

Envy is sadness at another's good, as if that good were an affront to one's superiority. As the rich are avaricious, so the poor are sometimes envious. The envious person hates to see anyone else happy. The charm, the beauty, the knowledge, the peace, the wealth of others are all regarded as having been purloined from him. Envy induces ugly women to make nasty remarks about beautiful women, and makes the stupid malign the wise. Since the envious person cannot go up, he tries to achieve equality by pulling the other down. Envy is always a snob, is always jealous and possessive. To the envious, all who are polite are castigated as "high-hat"; the religious they dub "hypocrites"; the well-bred "put on airs"; the learned are "high-brow". Envy begins by asking, "Why shouldn't I have everything that others have?" and ends by saying, "It is because others have these virtues that I do not have them." Then envy becomes enmity; it is devoid of respect and honor, and, above all, it can never say "Thank you" to anyone.

Envy begins its course by seeking to lower the reputation of another, either secretly, by talebearing and gossip, or overtly, by detraction. These succeeding, the term of envy is reached when there is joy at another's misfortune and when there is grief at another's success. When envy attacks another's spiritual progress or apostolic success, it is a grave matter.

One of the most effective ways of counteracting jealousy and envy in ourselves is to say a prayer immediately for the intention of the person we resent. By referring our enemies to God and by spiritually wishing them well, we crush the psychological impulse toward envy. A second means is to try to emulate those who provoke our envy: the Church holds up the good example of the saints, not to depress us, but to impress us—not to discourage us in our failings, but to encourage us to greater efforts. "Let us keep one another in mind, always ready with incitements to charity and to acts of piety" (Heb 10:24).

Lust is an inordinate love of the pleasures of the flesh. It is the prostitution of love, the extension of self-love to a point where the ego is projected into another person and loved under the illusion that the "thou" itself is being loved. Real love is directed toward a person, who is seen as irreplaceable and as unique; but lust excludes all personal consideration for the sake of sensate experience. The ego mislabels lust with modern tags, pretending that such a sin is required for "health" or for a "full life" or to "express the self".

Lust is a shifting of the center of personality from the spirit to the flesh, from the I to the ego. In some instances, its excesses are born of an uneasy conscience and of a desire to escape from self toward others; sometimes there is a contrary desire to make the ego supreme by the subordination of others to itself. In its later stages, the libertine finds that neither release from self nor idolatry is possible for long; the soul is driven back to self and, therefore, to an inner hell. The effect of lust on the will is to develop a hatred of God and a denial of immortality. Excesses also deplete the source of spiritual energy to such an extent that one finally becomes incapable of calm judgment in any other field.

There is no passion which more quickly produces slavery than lust—as there is none whose perversions more quickly destroy the power of the intellect and the will. Excesses affect the reason in four ways: by perverting the *understanding* so that one becomes intellectually blind and unable to see the truth; by weakening *prudence* and a sense of values, thus producing rashness; by building up self-love to generate *thoughtlessness*; by weakening the will until the power of decision is lost and one becomes a prey to *inconstancy* of character.

Anger is a violent desire to punish others. Here we refer not to righteous anger, such as that of Our Lord when He drove the buyers and sellers out of the temple, but the wrong kind of anger, which expresses itself in temper, vindictiveness, tantrums, revenge, and the clenching of the fist. Anger's disguise in the egotist's eyes is the desire to "get even" or "not to let him get away with it". In the press and on the platform anger calls itself "righteous indignation"; but underneath, it is still a mania to exploit wrath, to malign, and to foment grievances. Anger is very common among those with bad consciences; thieves will become far angrier when accused of theft than any honest man; unfaithful spouses will fly into a rage when caught in infidelity; women guilty of jealousy and malice "take it out" on their employees in the home. Those who displease such egoists are repulsed violently, and the good who reproach them by the pattern of their virtue are viciously maligned.

There are various degrees of anger; the first is touchiness—undue sensitiveness and impatience at the least slight. Because the coffee is cold at breakfast, or because the morning paper is late, the impatient ego nags and grumbles. The second stage is a flaring up of the temper, with violent gesticulation, blood boiling, redness of the face, and even the throwing of things; all of these are indications that the ego will brook no interference in the fulfillment of its selfish desires. The third and final stage is reached when there is physical violence directed against another—when hatred seeks to "get even" either by doing harm to another person or else by desiring his death. Many a man does not realize how much diabolical anger there is in him until his ego is aroused. Anger prevents the development of personality and halts all spiritual progress—not only because it disturbs mental poise and good judgment, but because it blinds to the rights of others and disturbs that spirit of recollection which is so necessary for compliance with the inspirations of grace.

Anger is always related to some frustration of the ego. It is particularly difficult to cure in others because it is rooted in self-love, although no egotist will admit that this is the cause. He would rather have his body hurt than his ego humiliated by such a meek acknowledgment.

Gluttony is an abuse of the lawful pleasure that God has attached to eating and drinking, which are a necessary means of self-preservation. It is an inordinate indulgence in the pleasures of eating and drinking, either by taking more than is necessary or by taking it at the wrong time or in too luxurious a manner. Gluttony disguises itself as "the good life", or as "the sophisticated way", or as "gracious living". An overstuffed, double-chinned generation takes gluttony for granted, rarely considering it a sin.

The malice in excessive love of eating and drinking comes from the fact that it enslaves the soul to the body and thus tends to weaken the moral and intellectual life of man.

Sloth is a malady of the will which causes neglect of one's duty. In the physical realm it appears as laziness, softness, idleness, procrastination, nonchalance, and indifference; as a spiritual disease, it takes the form of a distaste of the spiritual, lukewarmness at prayers, and contempt of self-discipline. Sloth is the sin of those who only look at picture-magazines, but never at print; who read only novels, but never a philosophy of life. Sloth disguises itself as tolerance and broad-mindedness—it has not enough intellectual energy to discover truth and follow it. Sloth loves nothing, hates nothing, hopes nothing, fears nothing, keeps alive because it sees nothing to die for. It rusts out rather than wears out; it would not render a service to any employer a minute after a whistle blows; and the more it increases in our midst, the more burdens it throws upon the state. Sloth is egocentrical; it is basically an attempt to escape from social and spiritual responsibilities, in the expectation that someone else will care for us. The lazy man is a parasite. He demands that others cater to him and earn his bread for him; he is asking special privileges in wishing to eat bread which he has not earned.

Self-examination always bears on one or another of these seven basic egotisms. It is hard to bear—the ego is reluctant to have itself examined. We tend to cheat ourselves through flattery: David begged God to search his heart, knowing that if he did it himself he would overlook serious sins. But self-knowing is rewarding, for these two things go together: self-revelation and God-revelation. The more a person discovers himself the way he really *is*, the more he feels the need of God, and the more God manifests Himself to such a soul. He becomes singlehearted, easy to understand. The less a person knows himself, the more complex he is: a mind into which self-analysis has never penetrated has a thousand unrelated motives and concerns. Its complexity is due to a want of inner penetration and the failure to bring all things to a focus in a single human goal.

"I have a bad temper", or "I drink too much", "I am always criticizing", or "I am lazy" are familiar complaints from those who still believe that nobility of character is an important goal. They would not make such admissions if they did not have a strong desire to break the chain of evil habits. They can realize this desire—any bad habit can be broken. But getting free of it requires four things:

Introspection is necessary in order that we shall isolate the habit and see it clearly as a sin. The surprise we feel when others criticize some fault in us proves that we have not practiced introspection sufficiently to know ourselves. Some people are afraid even to look into their consciences, for fear of what they might find; they are like the other cowards who dare not open telegrams because they dread bad news. But introspection is to the soul what diagnosis is to the body—the first necessary step toward health. The Prodigal Son "entered into himself" before he was able to resolve to admit his mistakes to his father. Turning the searchlight of attention upon ourselves shows us the vice or evil habit which requires correction; it makes us see ourselves not as we wish we were, but as we really are.

Avoiding the occasions of sin is the easiest way of avoiding sin itself. The way to keep out of trouble is to keep out of situations that lead up to trouble: the man who gets burned whenever he is near a fire had better eschew fires. The alcoholic must avoid the first sip of the first drink; the libertine must keep away from pretty women; the evil-minded must flee the company of those who degrade him. Our Lord said, "He that loveth the danger will perish therein." Temptation is hard to overcome at the last moment, when the sin is within our reach; it is easy to overcome if we act decisively to avoid a situation in which we might be tempted. Environments can make sin repulsive or attractive to us, for our surroundings affect us all. But we can *choose* the environment we wish and can ruthlessly reject the one that leads to trouble. Our Lord told us, "If thy right eye is the occasion of thy falling into sin, pluck it out and cast it away from thee." This means that if the books we read, the homes we visit, the games we play cause us to stumble morally, then we should cut them out and cast them from us.

An act of the will is vital to any accomplishment. Doctors tell us that nothing is a greater help to the sick man than a will to live. So if we are to overcome our vices, we must bring a strong will to bear on them. We acquired the bad habits only because we gave ground to them by a consent of the will until they became automatic and perhaps even unconscious. To master them, we must reverse the process and use the will to break their automatic functioning. Our characters do not consist in what we know, but in what we choose, and choosing is done by the will. After the Prodigal had entered into himself and left the environment of sin, his next stop was to brace himself with the great resolve, "I will arise and go to my father."

A right philosophy of life is needed to complete the work, for evil habits cannot be overcome by the will alone: love is required as well. No alcoholic is cured until he finds something to value more highly than the attractions of alcohol. No other evil is renounced until the sinner finds some positive good he prizes above his sin. Our Lord warned us of the house, swept and garnished, which was filled by seven devils worse than the first; this was the inevitable result when an evil was driven out and no good was sent to take its place. Even in the moral world, nature abhors a vacuum.

Evil habits are not driven out by our hate of them (for we do not always hate them properly). They are crowded out by our love of something else. The new love that takes possession of us must be bigger than ourselves—for it is ourselves which need amendment. It cannot safely be anything easy that we use as a substitute love; the man who cures himself of dissipation through pride or ambition may be worse off, in his reform, than in his sin. No new, competing love is large enough except the love of God Himself, with all that that love makes us long to do. St. Augustine summarized its effects when he said, "Love God, and do what you will." For if you love God truly, you will never wish to hurt Him, any more than you would wish to hurt a human friend.

Habits cannot be efficaciously fought unless we have a philosophy which makes our lives revolve around the God for Whom we are made, and without Whom we are miserably bound to the drab companionship of our own growing imperfections.

The most interesting tax collector in the history of the world was Zacchaeus—if you can call any tax collector "interesting". Physically he was so short that whenever there was a parade, he always had to climb a tree in order to see it. His name meant "pure", but he was anything but that, for he was a "twenty-five per center", always taking that much at least out of what he collected for his "cut". But the end of the story reveals that he was much better than his neighbors believed him to be.

This particular day Our Blessed Lord came to the village, and Zacchaeus, as was his wont, climbed a sycamore tree. People that want for size must make up for it by sagacity. Not many tax collectors in our days, particularly those who are rich, as was Zacchaeus, would humble themselves by elevating themselves in a tree. But Zacchaeus was rewarded, for Our Lord saw him and He asked him to take Him home. Whenever the Lord wants to give a favor, He often asks for one.

When the door was closed behind the two of them, the mob outside was angry, not with the tax collector because

he was dishonest, but they were angry with Our Divine
Lord because He ate with disreputable people and sinners.
The Savior's way of looking at it was that He had found
one sheep that went astray. After a few minutes the conscience of the tax collector was aroused—for consciences
only sleep, they never die. Zacchaeus promised to make
amends for his dishonesty by giving half of his goods
to the poor and restoring fourfold to anyone whom he
had cheated.

Restitution is a duty which a civilization which stresses
profits and money can readily forget. When anyone has
been cheated, when capitalists underpay their workers,
when labor leaders during a strike pour gasoline into milk
destined for hospitals, when radio and television repair
men pile up needless expenses by a seeming substitution
of one tube for another, when an honest day's work is
not given for an honest day's pay, there is no distribution
of that equilibrium and balance of justice which makes
the world livable. Remorse is not enough; shame is not
enough. The balming of dishonesty by saying one has an
Oedipus complex, or that one feared his grandmother are
not enough. There must be a restoring of the property
that was stolen. If the person who was cheated cannot be
found, there must be a donation of an equal amount to
the poor. Restitution is the restoring of a person to that
condition from which, contrary to right and duty, we have
removed him.

The reason for rendering satisfaction for our dishonesty
is clear. The law of nature and the law of the land affirm
that every man ought to possess in undisturbed use those
goods to which he has a right. If we steal something from
our neighbor at nine o'clock at night, it does not rightfully
become ours at ten o'clock. In other words, the passing
of time does not change the right, nor make lawful that

which was unlawful. Under the Levitical Law, the Jews were obliged to give "five oxen for an ox, and four sheep for a sheep". Time never cancels out the duty of restoring that which we may have had for the theft. The proof that we are sorry is that we return the stolen goods.

To make money dishonestly and then put it in the wife's name is not to escape the obligation to make restitution. Since such a person never owned the property lawfully, he never could make the transfer legally. Suppose a man is sold a handkerchief on the pretense that it is silk, when really it is nylon—restitution must be made. A secondhand-car dealer who tells a buyer that the car is in perfect condition, and yet knows that he filled the rear transmission with sawdust to hide for a hundred miles the defective gears— such a crook is bound to make restitution.

There is a story—and it is only a story—about a man who went to confession. During confession he stole the priest's watch. He then told the priest that he had stolen a watch. The priest said: "You must make restitution." The thief said: "I will give it to you, Father." "No," said the priest, "give it to the owner." The penitent then said: "The owner won't take it back." "In that case," said the priest, "you can keep it."

If this were not a story, the penitent would still be bound to make restitution—not only to man, but also to God. Honesty is not a policy, it is a duty!

6

Christian Marriage and Love

Love is primarily in the will, not in the emotions or the glands. The will is like the voice; the emotions are like the echo. The *pleasure* associated with love, or what is today called "sex", is the frosting on the cake; its purpose is to make us love the cake, not ignore it. The greatest illusion of lovers is to believe that the intensity of their sexual attraction is the guarantee of the perpetuity of their love. It is because of this failure to distinguish between the glandular and spiritual—or between sex which we have in common with animals, and love which we have in common with God—that marriages are so full of deception. What some people love is not a person, but the experience of being in love. Love is irreplaceable; sex is not. To the Christian, sex is inseparable from the person, and to reduce the person to sex is as silly as to reduce personality to lungs or a thorax. Certain Victorians in their education practically denied sex as a function of personality; certain sexophiles of modern times deny personality and make a god of sex. The male animal is attracted to the female animal, but a human personality is attracted to another human personality. The attraction of beast to beast is physiological; the attraction of human to human is physiological, psychological, and spiritual.

Sex in isolation from personality does not exist! An arm living and gesticulating apart from the living organism is an impossibility. Man has no organic functions isolated from his soul. There is involvement of the whole personality. Nothing is more psychosomatic than the union of two in one flesh; nothing so much alters a mind, a will, for better or for worse. The separation of soul and body is death. Those who separate sex and spirit are rehearsing for death. The enjoyment of the other's personality through one's own personality is love. The pleasure of animal function through another's animal function is sex separated from love.

But when sex is divorced from love there is a feeling that one has been stopped at the vestibule of the castle of pleasure; that the heart has been denied the city after crossing the bridge. Sadness and melancholy result from such a frustration of destiny, for it is the nature of man to be sad when he is pulled outside himself, or exteriorized without getting any nearer his goal. There is a closer correlation between mental instability and the animal view of sex than many suspect.

He who spends his energy on the external without understanding its mystery is unhappy to the point of melancholy. There is the feeling of being hungry after having eaten, or of being disgusted with food, because it has nourished not the body, in the case of an individual, or another body, in the case of marriage. In the woman, this sadness is due to the humiliation of realizing that where marriage is only sex, her role could be fulfilled by any other woman; there is nothing personal, incommunicable, and therefore nothing dignified. Summoned by her God-implanted nature to be ushered into the mysteries of life which have their source in God, she is condemned to remain on the threshold as a tool or an instrument of pleasure alone, and not as a companion of love. Two glasses that are empty cannot fill up one another. There must be a fountain of water outside the glasses, in order that they may have communion with one another. It takes *three* to make love.

Love is directed to someone else for the sake of the other's perfection; sex is directed to self for the sake of self-satisfaction. Sex flatters the object not because it is praiseworthy in itself, but rather as a solicitation. The ego in sex pleads that it loves the alter ego, but what it loves is really the possibility of its own pleasure in the other ego. The other person is necessary for the return of the egotist upon himself. But love, which stresses the object, finds itself in constantly enlarging relationships. Love is so strong it surpasses narrowness by devotedness and forgetfulness of self.

Sex is moved by the desire to fill a moment between having and not having. It is an experience like looking at a sunset, or twirling one's thumbs to pass the time. It rests after one experience, because glutted for the moment, and then waits for the reappearance of a new craving or passion to be satisfied on a totally different object. Love frowns upon this notion, for it sees in this nothing but the killing of the objects loved for the sake of self-satisfaction. Sex would give birds flight, but no nests; it would give hearts emotions but no homes; throw the whole world into the experience of voyagers at sea, but with no ports. Instead of pursuing an Infinite which is fixed, it substitutes the false infinity of never finding satisfaction. The infinite then becomes not the possession of love but the fruitless search for love, which is the basis of so many psychoses and neuroses. The infinite then becomes restlessness, a merry-go-round of the heart which spins only to spin again.

Real love, on the contrary, admits the need, the thirst, the passion, the craving, but it also admits an abiding satisfaction by adhesion to a value which transcends time and

space. Love unites itself to being and thus becomes perfect; sex unites itself to non-being and thus becomes irrita-
tion and anxiety. In love, poverty becomes integrated into
riches; need into fulfillment; yearning into joy; chase into
capture. But sex is without the joy of offering. The wolf
offers nothing when he kills the lamb. The joy of oblation
is missing, for the egotist by his very nature seeks inflation.
Love gives to receive. Sex receives so as not to give. Love
is soul contact with another for the sake of perfection; sex is
body contact with another for the sake of sublimation.

God did not intend that strength in a man and beauty in
a woman should endure, but that they should reappear
in their children. Here is where God's providence reveals
itself. Just at a time when it might seem that beauty is
fading in one, and strength in the other, God sends children to protect and revive both. When the first boy is
born, the husband reappears in all his strength and promise
and, in the language of Virgil, "from high heaven descends
a worthier race of men". When the first girl is born, the
wife revives in all her beauty and charm, and even the baby
talk becomes cute all over again. He even likes to think
that she is the sole source of the daughter's loveliness. Each
child that is born begins to be a bead in the great rosary of
love, binding the parents together in the rosy chains of a
sweet slavery of love.

No self-loathing, satiety, and fear seize their souls, for
they never pluck the fruit of love at its core nor break the
lute to snare the music. Love becomes an ascension from
the sense-plane through an incarnation and rises back again
to God, as they train their children for their native heaven
and its Trinity, whence came their sparks of fire and love.
From the time the children learn to bless themselves and
say the name of Jesus, through that hour when they learn

in little catechisms greater truths than the worldly-wise could give, to that day when they themselves start love again on its pilgrimage, the parents have a consciousness of their trusteeship under God.

Purity is reverence paid to the mystery of sex. In every mystery, there are two elements: one visible, the other invisible. For example, in Baptism, water is the visible element, the regenerating grace of Christ is the invisible element. Sex is a mystery, too, because it has these two characteristics. Sex is something known to everyone, and yet it is something hidden from everyone. The known element is that everyone is either male or female. The invisible, hidden, mysterious element in sex is its capacity for *creativeness*, a sharing in some way of the creative power by which God made the world and all that is in it. As God's love is the creative principle of the universe, so God willed that the love of man and woman should be the creative principle of the family. This power of human beings to beget one made to their image and likeness is something like God's creative power, inasmuch as it is related to freedom; for God's own creative act was free.

Breathing, digestion, and circulation are to a great extent unconscious and involuntary. These processes go on independently of our wills, but our power to "create" either a poem, a statue, or a child, is free. In that moment when freedom was born, God said: "Creatures, create yourselves." This divine commission to "increase and multiply" new life through love is a communication of the power by which God created all life.

The mystery of creativeness is surrounded with awe. A special reverence does envelop the power to be co-creators with God in the making of human life. It is this hidden element which in a special way belongs to God, as does the grace of God in the sacraments. Those who speak of sex alone concentrate on the physical or visible element, forgetting the spiritual or invisible mystery of creativeness. Humans in the sacraments supply the act, the bread, the water, and the words; God supplies the grace, the mystery. In the sacred act of creating life, man and woman supply the unity of the flesh; God supplies the soul and the mystery. Such is the mystery of sex.

In youth, this awesomeness before the mystery manifests itself in a woman's timidity, which makes her shrink from a precocious or too ready surrender of her secret. In a man, the mystery is revealed in chivalry to women, not because he believes that woman is physically weaker, but because of the awe he feels in the presence of mystery. Because, too, of the reverence which envelops this mysterious power which came from God, mankind has always felt that it is to be used only by a special sanction from God and under certain relationships. That is why, traditionally, marriage has been associated with religious rites, to bear witness to the fact that the power of sex, which comes from God, should have its use approved by God because it is destined to fulfill His creative designs.

Purity, then, is not mere physical intactness. In the woman, it is a firm resolve never to use the power until God shall send her a husband. In the man, it is a steadfast desire to wait upon God's will that he have a wife, for the use of God's purpose. Purity does not begin in the body, but in the will. From there it flows outward, cleansing thought, imagination, and, finally, the body. Bodily purity is a repercussion or echo of the will. Life is impure only when the will is impure.

Purity is first psychical before it is physical. It is first in the mind and heart, and then overflows to the body. In this it differs from hygiene. Hygiene is concerned with a *fait accompli*; purity, with an attitude before the act. Our Lord said: "But I tell you that he who casts his eyes on a woman so as to lust after her has already committed adultery with her in his heart" (Mt 5:28). Our Savior did not wait until the thought became the deed but entered into a conscience to brand even a thought impure. If the rivers that pour into the sea are clean, the sea itself will be clean. If it is wrong to do a certain thing, it is wrong to think about that thing. Purity is reverent inwardness, not biological intactness. It is not something private, but rather something secret which is not to be "told" until it is God-approved.

Purity is a consciousness that each possesses a gift which can be *given* only once, and can be *received* only once. In the unity of flesh he makes her a woman; she makes him a man. They may enjoy the gift many times, but once given it can never be taken back, either in man or in woman. It is not just a physiological experience, but the unraveling of a mystery. As one can pass just once from ignorance to knowledge of a given point, for example, the principle of contradiction, so one can pass just once from incompleteness to the full knowledge of self which the partner brings. Once that border line is crossed, neither belongs wholly to self. Their reciprocity has created dependence; the riddle has been solved, the mystery has been revealed; the dual have become a unity, either sanctioned by God or in defiance of His will.

God could not make the earth and the fullness thereof without love; Mary could not conceive in her womb without love. She did conceive without human love, but not without divine love. Though fragmentary human passion was lacking, divine love was not, for the angel said to her: "The Holy Spirit will come upon thee, and the power of the most High will overshadow thee" (Lk 1:35). Since purity is reverence for the mystery of creativeness, who was more pure than the woman who bore the creator of creativeness and who in the ecstasy of that love could say to the world in the language of G. K. Chesterton: "In thy house lust without love shall die. In my house love without lust shall live"?

Because purity is reverence for the mystery of creativeness, it has its range from the child to the youth, from the altar to the home, from the widowed to the consecrated, differing in degrees but not in the sublime consciousness that there must be a divine permission to lift the veil of the mystery. Because purity is the guardian of love, the Church bids all her children look to Mary as their protectress and model. Mary is the abstraction of love from love; the soft halo of the love of Jesus; the hearth of His flame; the ark of His life. Because she kept her secret until the fullness of her time had come with the Angel's announcement, she became the hope of those who are tempted to premature exploitation of the mystery. There is no class or condition of souls she does not teach that bodily purity is the echo of the will.

As Francis Thompson wrote:

> But Thou, who knowest the hidden thing
> Thou hast instructed me to sing,
> Teach Love the way to be
> A new Virginity.
>
> Do Thou with Thy protecting hand
> Shelter the flame thy breath has fanned;
> Let my heart's reddened glow
> Be but as sun flushed snow.
>
> And if they say that snow is cold,
> O Chastity, must they be told
> The hand that's chafed with snow
> Takes a redoubled glow?—

That extreme cold like heat doth sear?
O to the heart of love draw near,
And feel how scorching rise
Its white cold purities.

But Thou, sweet Lady Chastity,
Thou, and Thy brother Love with thee,
Upon her lap may'st still
Sustain me, if you will.

Pregnancy becomes illumined by mystery as the pro-
spective mother hears the chant of the liturgy: *Non hor-
ruisti Virginis uterum.* "Thou hast not despised the womb of
a woman." Every descent of new life into the body of a
woman is possible only because God has infused the soul
into the child by a creative act. The child is not the person of God, as it was within the womb of the Virgin, but
it is nevertheless the act of God, which is present within
her. Nowhere within creation does God more intimately
cooperate with a human than in the generation of life. The
liturgy, speaking of Mary's pregnancy, says: "He whom
the heavens could not contain, thou didst contain within
thyself." So the mother whose model is the Mother of
Mothers sees herself as bearing within her the creative act
of God, which not even the universe can limit.

When, as a bride, she went to the altar, the Church
said to her and her husband: "You will be two in one
flesh." Looking to the Incarnation, she perceives in a dim
way that such must have been Mary's thought as she bore
within herself the Word Incarnate. She and her Son were
two in one flesh, the symbol of matrimony. In Mary,
the sexes were reconciled, and a woman and a man were
one. Now, bearing the child, the mother sees how the
unity of two in one flesh, which existed between her

and her husband, passes into a new unity of two in one flesh: herself and her unborn child.

Mothers who know not the spirit in sex can see themselves only as more-highly developed animals, bearing within a new biological content. But the Catholic mother finds a model of pregnancy in the Mother who began the bringing of God to man. Physical trials become more bearable when she sees herself a co-worker with God in the making of life. A dying man in a country region of France, unable to receive the Eucharist, asked that a poor person be brought to him so that he might at least have Christ in a lesser way. The woman with the child may sometimes be unable to receive Holy Communion, but she can, with an act of faith, see that she already is bearing a lesser host within the tabernacle of her body.

Nowhere does Sacred Scripture speak of marriage in terms of sex. Instead, it speaks of it in terms of knowledge. "And now Adam had knowledge of his wife, Eve, and she conceived. She called her child Cain, as if she would say, Canithi, I have been enriched by the Lord with a man-child" (Gen 4:1). And when the Angel Gabriel announced to the Blessed Virgin that she was chosen to be the Mother of God, Mary asked: "How can that be, since I have no knowledge of man?" (Lk 1:34). There was no question here of ignorance of conception but of some deeper mystery. Marriage is here related to knowledge. The closest union that exists between anything in the universe and man himself is through knowledge. When the mind knows *flower* and *tree*, man possesses these objects within his intellect. They are not identified with his intellect, but are distinct from it. These objects exist inside the mind in a new manner of being. An object outside the mind thus exists inside the mind as well, and without ceasing to be itself. This union of the object and the mind, or the thing known and the knower, is one of the closest unions possible in the natural order.

Sacred Scripture speaks of marriage as knowledge, because it represents a union much more profound and lasting, much more bound up with our psychic structure, than the mere biological unity that comes from the mating of animals.

Because marriage is knowledge, it follows that its unity is one which demands fidelity. Suppose a student never knew, until he entered college, the soliloquy of Hamlet. Once he had come to *know* that, which he never knew before, he would always be *dependent* on the college which had given him that knowledge. That is why he calls that college his "beloved mother", his *alma mater*. It caused something to happen to him which was unique. He could go on enjoying the soliloquy all the days of his life, but he could never re-acquire it. So, too, when man and woman come to the knowledge of another person, when they, as rational creatures, establish a unity in the flesh which before they never knew; they can go on enjoying that knowledge, but they never can re-acquire it. So long as time endures, he gave to her the knowledge of man, and she gave to him the knowledge of woman. And they gave knowledge because they gave unity, not of object and mind, but of flesh and flesh. Others can repeat the knowledge, even unlawfully, but there was always someone who was the first to unfold the mystery of life.

Thus the union between husband and wife is not an experience that may be forgotten. It is a knowledge or an identity that has permanence about it. They are "two in one flesh". From this point of view, there is nothing that happens to a woman that does not happen to man; the accidents of the union are only a symbol of a real change

that has occurred in both. Neither can live again as if
nothing had ever happened. There is a kind of ontological
bond established between the two which is related, though
not in the same order, as the bond between a mother and
her child. By the very nature of things, only one person
can bring this knowledge to another. This already suggests
a union that is more personal than carnal. No one minds
eating in public, because there is not a personal union
of the food and the stomach. But making love in public
is vulgar because, by its very nature, love is personal. It
exists between two persons, and only two, and therefore
resents intrusion or vulgarity. Their love is spoiled when
others know it, and so marriage is spoiled when a third
knows its secret.

The unification from the duality of flesh of husband and
wife is one of the reasons why the Savior forbade the breaking of the bond. Both men and women, in the moment
of the *knowing*, receive a gift which neither ever knew
before, and which they can never know again except by
repetition. The resulting psychic changes are as great as the
somatic. The woman can never return again to virginity;
the man can never return again to ignorance. Something
has happened to make them one, and from that oneness
comes fidelity, so long as either has a body.

Human generation is not a push upward from the beast,
but rather a gift downward from the Trinity. The begetting of children is not an imitation of the beasts of the
field, but a feeble reflection of the eternal generation of
the Second Person in the bosom of the Father.

This brings us to the first law of Love: *All love ends in an
incarnation, even God's.* Love would not be love if it did not
escape the limitations of individual existence by perpetu-
ating itself, nor if it did not achieve a kind of immortality

in progeny, wherein death is defeated by life. Behind the urge to procreate is the hidden desire of every human to participate in the eternal. Since man cannot do this in himself, he compensates for it by continuing life in another. Our inability to eternalize ourselves is overcome by giving, with God's help, something immortal to the human race.

The act of generation, when seen as the gift of God and performed in the state of grace or love of God, merits for husband and wife further graces and helps them to save their souls. As St. Thomas puts it: "If one is led to perform the marriage act either by virtue of justice, in order to render the debt to the partner, or by virtue of religion, that children may be procreated for the worship of God, the act is meritorious."

But the begetting of new life is a sign that the heart is so full of happiness and love that it will die unless it overflows. The choked and dammed river collects scum and dirt, but the quick mountain streams that hurry over sacrificial rocks are purified in their flight to bedew newer and richer fields. Man is not made for isolation, neither is he made for collectivity; but he is made for the living group, the family, the community, the nation, and the Church. To live in it, however, he must contribute to it: husband and wife by physical birth, the priest by spiritual birth or conversion. For body and soul, therefore, generation is the condition of wholeness, sanity, and order. The priest who begets no new life in Christ, whether through his preaching, his sacrifices, his mortifications, or his actual conversions, is condemning himself to the same penalties of sterility as do the husband and wife who rebel against the law of life.

There is no disgust in a life that is fecund, because there is a mystery. As time goes on, the river of rapture of husband and wife broadens. The eddies of passion may

remain in the shallows, but their current never stops flowing. The companionship that began in ecstasies of flesh
now widens into the sharing of bread, the communion of
mind and heart and will, as they taste the sweet delirium
of simply being together. Love is soon discovered to be
oneness, more than the mere assimilation at which new
lovers strain. The glamor passes, but the mystery deepens
until they are made one through the deep sharing of life's
meaning in the mystery of an eternal love that gave only
to receive.

If human love does not always continue as an ecstatic
joy, it is because God has kept something back, namely,
Himself in eternity. So He makes everyone run up against
a stone wall every now and then in life; on such occasions
they feel the crisis of nonentity and have an overwhelming sense of nothingness and loneliness, in order that they
may see life not as a city but as a bridge to eternity. The
crisis of nothingness is caused by the meeting of a fancied
ideal and reality; of love as the ego thinks it is, and of love
as it really is.

During this crisis of nothingness, the things that hearts
are kicking and complaining against are not their destiny,
nor their nature, but their limits, their weaknesses, their
insufficiency. The human heart is not wrong in wanting
love; it is wrong only in thinking that a human can completely supply it. What the soul yearns for in the crisis is the
light of love, which is God, and not the shadow. The crisis
of nothingness is a summons to the everything which is
God. The abyss of one's own poverty cries out to the abyss
of the infinite richness of divine love. Instead of thinking
that the other partner is to blame for this emptiness, which
is so common today, one ought to peer into his own soul.
He wants the ocean, and he is drinking from a cup. If
there is a thorn in the flesh at this moment of life, as Our

Lord gave a thorn to the flesh of Paul for the purpose of purification, the thorn is a summons to climb to the flame of love which is God.

What the dark night of the soul is to the spiritual life, the dark night of the body is to marriage. Neither is permanent; both are occasions of purification for fresher insights into Love. If the fig tree of love is to bear fruit, it must be purged and dunged. Dryness in the spiritual life and in marriage are really actual graces. God's finger is stirring the waters of the soul, creating discontent, that new efforts may be put forth. As the mother eagle throws its young out of the nest, in order that they may fly, so now God is giving love its wings in place of its clay feet.

In the days of romance, the eternal emphasis was on the ego's durability in love; in the crisis of nothingness, the eternal element is God, not the ego. Love now says, "I will love you always, for you are lovable through eternity for God's sake." He who courts and promises eternal love is actually appropriating to himself an attribute of God. During the dark night of the body, he puts eternity where it rightly belongs, namely, in God.

Once purified, love returns. The partner is loved beyond all sensation, all desire, all concupiscence. The husband who began by loving the other for his own sake, and then for her sake, now begins to love for God's sake. He has touched the depths of a body, but now he discovers the soul of the other person. This is the new infinite taking the place of the body; this is the new "always", and it is closer to the true infinite because the soul is infinite and spiritual, whereas the body is not. The other partner ceases to be opaque and begins to be transparent, the glass through which God and His purposes are revealed. Less conscious of his own power to beget love in others, he sees his poverty and begins to depend on God to complement that poverty. Good Friday now passes into Easter Sunday with the Resurrection of love.

Love, which once meant pleasure and self-satisfaction, changes into love for God's sake. The other person becomes less the necessary condition of passion and more the partner of the soul. Our Blessed Lord said that unless the seed fall to the ground and die, it will not spring forth into life. Nothing is reborn to a higher life without a death in the lower. The heart has its cycles as do the planets, but the movement of the heart is an upward spiral, and not a circle which turns upon itself. The planetary circles are repetitious; the eternal return to a beginning.

What if the husband becomes an alcoholic or unfaithful or beats his wife and children? What if the wife becomes nagging or unfaithful or neglects her children?

Suppose the promise of marriage "for better or for worse" turns out for the worse; suppose either husband or wife becomes a chronic invalid, or develops antisocial characteristics. In such cases, no carnal love can save it. It is even difficult for a personal love to save it, particularly if the other party becomes undeserving. But when these lower loves break down, Christian love steps in to suggest that the other person is to be regarded as a *gift* of God. Most of God's gifts are sweet; a few of them, however, are bitter. But whether that other person be bitter or sweet, sick or well, young or old, he or she is still a gift of God, for whom the other partner must sacrifice himself or herself. Selfish love would seek to get rid of the other person because he is a burden. Christian love takes on the burden, in obedience to the divine command: "Bear the burden of one another's failings; then you will be fulfilling the law of Christ" (Gal 6:2).

And if it be objected that God never intended that anyone should live under such difficulties, the answer very flatly is that He does: "If any man has a mind to come my way, let him renounce self, and take up his cross, and follow me. The man who tries to save his life shall lose it; it is the man who loses his life for my sake that will secure it" (Mt 16:24, 25). What sickness is to an individual, an unhappy marriage may be to a couple: a trial sent by God in order to perfect them spiritually. Without some of the bitter gifts of God, many of our spiritual capacities would be undeveloped. As the Holy Word of God tells us: "We are confident even over our afflictions, knowing well that affliction gives rise to endurance, and endurance gives proof of our faith, and a proved faith gives ground for hope. Nor does this hope delude us; the love of God has been poured out in our hearts by the Holy Spirit, whom we have received" (Rom 5:3–5).

Christian love, on the part of one spouse, will help redeem the other partner. If a father will pay his son's debts to keep him out of prison, if a man will give a blood transfusion to save his friend's life, then it is possible in a spouse.

As the Scriptures tell us: "The unbelieving husband is sanctified by the believing wife; and the unbelieving wife is sanctified by the believing husband" (1 Cor 7:14). This is one of the most forgotten texts on the subject of marriage. It applies to the spiritual order the common experiences of the physical. If a husband is ill, the wife will nurse him back to health. In the spiritual order, the one who has faith and love of God will take on the burdens of the unbeliever, such as drunkenness, infidelity, and mental cruelty, for the sake of his soul. What a blood transfusion is to the body, reparation for the sins of another is to the spirit. Instead of separating when there are difficulties and trials, the Christian solution is to bear the other as a cross for the sake of his sanctification. The wife can redeem the husband, and the husband the wife.

This transferability of sanctification from a good wife to a bad husband, or from a good husband to a bad wife, follows from the fact that they are two in one flesh. As skin can be grafted from the back to the face, so merit can be applied from spouse to spouse. This spiritual communication may not have the romantic satisfaction in it that carnal communication has, but its returns are eternal. Many a husband and wife after infidelities and excesses will find themselves saved on Judgment Day, as the faithful partner never ceased to pour out prayers for his or her salvation.

7

Prayer and Meditation

The essence of prayer is not the effort to make God give us something—as this is not the basis of sound human friendships—but there is a legitimate prayer of petition. God has two kinds of gifts: first, there are those which He sends us whether we pray for them or not; and the second kind are those which are given on condition that we pray. The first gifts resemble those things which a child receives in a family—food, clothing, shelter, care, and watchfulness. These gifts come to every child, whether the child asks for them or not. But there are other gifts, which are conditioned upon the desire of the child. A father may be eager to have a son go to college, but if the boy refuses to study or becomes a delinquent, the gift which the father intended for him can never be bestowed. It is not because the father has retracted his gift, but rather because the son has made the gift impossible. Of the first kind of gifts Our Blessed Lord spoke when He said: "His rain falls on the just and equally on the unjust" (Mt 5:45). He spoke of the second kind of gifts when He said: "Ask, and the gift will come."

Prayer, then, is not just the informing of God of our needs, for He already knows them. "You have a Father in heaven who knows that you need them all" (Mt 6:32). Rather, the purpose of prayer is to give Him the opportunity to bestow the gifts He will give us when we are ready to accept them. It is not the eye which makes the light of the sun surround us; it is not the lung which makes the air envelop us. The light of the sun is there if we do not close our eyes to it, and the air is there for our lungs if we do not hold our breath. God's blessings are there—if we do not rebel against His will to give.

The man who thinks only of himself says only prayers of petition; he who thinks of his neighbor says prayers of intercession; he who thinks only of loving and serving God, says prayers of abandonment to God's will, and this is the prayer of the saints. The price of this prayer is too high for most people, for it demands the displacement of our ego. Many souls want God to do *their* will; they bring their completed plans and ask Him to rubberstamp them without a change. The petition of the "Our Father" is changed by them to read: "*My* will be done on earth." It is very difficult for the Eternal to give Himself to those who are interested only in the temporal. The soul who lives on the ego-level or the I-level and refuses to be brought to the divine level is like an egg which is kept forever in a place too cool for incubation, so that it is never called upon to live a life outside of the shell of its own incomplete development. Every I is still an embryo of what a man is meant to be.

Where there is love, there is thought about the one we love. "Where your treasure-house is, there your heart is too" (Mt 6:21). The degree of our devotion and love depends upon the value that we put upon a thing: St. Augustine says, *Amor pondus meum*; love is the law of gravitation. All things have their center. The schoolboy finds it hard to study, because he does not love knowledge as much as athletics. The businessman finds it hard to think of heavenly pleasures because he is dedicated to the filling

of his "barn". The carnal-minded find it difficult to love
the spirit because their treasure lies in the flesh. Everyone
becomes like that which he loves: if he loves the material,
he becomes like the material; if he loves the spiritual, he is
converted into it in his outlook, his ideals, and his aspirations. Given this relationship between love and prayer, it is
easy to understand why some souls say: "I have no time to
pray." They really have not, because to them other duties
are more pressing, other treasures more precious, other
interests more exhilarating. As watches that are brought
too close to a dynamo cease to keep time, so, too, hearts
that become too much absorbed in external things soon
lose their capacity to pray. But as a jeweler with a mag-
net can draw the magnetism out of the watch and reset it
by the sky, so, too, it is possible to become de-egotized
by prayer, and be reset to the eternal and to love divine.

A higher form of prayer than petition—and a potent
remedy against the externalization of life—is meditation.
Meditation is a little like a daydream or a reverie, but
with two important differences: in meditation we do not
think about the world or ourselves, but about God. And
instead of using the imagination to build idle castles in
Spain, we use the will to make resolutions that will draw
us nearer to one of the Father's mansions. Meditation is a
more advanced spiritual act than "saying prayers"; it may
be likened to the attitude of a child who breaks into the
presence of a mother saying: "I'll not say a word, if you
will just let me stay here and watch you." Or, as a soldier
once told the Curé of Ars: "I just stand here before the
tabernacle; He looks at me and I look at Him."

Meditation allows one to suspend the conscious fight
against external diversions by an internal realization of the
presence of God. It shuts out the world to let in the Spirit.
It surrenders our own will to the impetus of the divine
will. It turns the searchlight of divine truth on the way

we think, act, and speak, penetrating beneath the layers of our self-deceit and egotism. It summons us before the bar of divine justice, so that we may see ourselves as we really are, and not as we like to think we are. It silences the ego with its clamorous demands, in order that it may hear the wishes of the divine heart. It uses our faculties, not to speculate on matters remote from God, but to stir up the will to conform more perfectly with His will. It cultivates a truly scientific attitude toward God as truth, freeing us from our prepossessions and our biases so that we may eliminate all wishful thinking from our minds.

It eliminates from our lives the things that would hinder union with God and strengthens our desire that all the good things we do shall be done for His Honor and Glory. It takes our eyes off the flux and change of life and reminds us of our *being*, the creatureliness, the dependence of all things on God for creation, moment-to-moment existence, and salvation. Meditation is not a petition, a way of using God, or asking things from Him, but rather a surrender, a plea to God that He use us.

For meditation the ear of the soul is more important than the tongue: St. Paul tells us that faith comes from listening. Most people commit the same mistake with God that they do with their friends: they do all the talking. Our Lord warned against those who "use many phrases, like the heathens, who think to make themselves heard by their eloquence" (Mt 6:7). One can be impolite to God, too, by absorbing all the conversation, and by changing the words of Scripture from "Speak, Lord, Thy servant hears" to "Listen, Lord, Thy servant speaks." God has things to tell us which will enlighten us—we must wait for Him to speak. No one would rush into a physician's office, rattle off all the symptoms, and then dash away without waiting for a diagnosis; no one would tune in the radio and immediately leave the room. It is every bit as stupid to ring God's

doorbell and then run away. The Lord hears us more readily than we suspect; it is our listening to Him that needs to
be improved. When people complain that their prayers are
not heard by God, what often has happened is that they
did not wait to hear His answer.

The best exposition of the steps in meditation is found
in the account of Easter Sunday in the Gospel. The disciples on that day were most forlorn. In their sadness they fell
into talk about Our Lord with a traveler whom they had
met by chance on the Emmaus road. This marks the first
stage of meditation: they spoke *about* Our Lord, not realizing He was present. This is followed by Our Lord's
disclosure of His presence—we listen, then, as the disciples did when He began to unfold to them the meaning
of His Passion and Death. Finally, there comes a stage of
communion—signified by the breaking of bread at supper
in the Gospel; at this point the soul is united to God, and
God to the soul. It is a moment one reluctantly abandons,
even when the day is far spent and fatigue is great.

Meditation improves our behavior. It is often stated that
it makes no difference what we believe, that all depends on
how we act; but this is meaningless, for we act upon our
beliefs. Hitler acted on the theory of Nazism and produced
a war; Stalin acted on the ideology of Marx and Lenin and
begot slavery. If our thoughts are bad, our actions will
also be bad. The problem of impure actions is basically
the problem of impure thoughts; the way to keep a man
from robbing a bank is to distract him from thinking about
robbing a bank. Political, social, and economic injustices
are, first, psychic evils—they originate in the mind. They
become social evils because of the intensity of the thought
that begot them.

Nothing ever happens in the world that does not first
happen inside a mind. Hygiene is no cure for immorality,
but if the wellsprings of thought were kept clean, there

would be no need to care for the effects of evil thinking on the body. When one meditates and fills his mind for an hour a day with thoughts and resolutions bearing on the love of God and neighbor above all things, there is a gradual seepage of love down to the level of what is called the subconscious, and finally these good thoughts emerge, of themselves, in the form of effortless good actions. Everyone has verified in his own life a thousand times the ideo-motor character of thought. Watching a football game, the spectator sees a player running with the ball; if there is a beautiful opening around right end, he may twist and turn his own body more than the runner does, to try to take advantage of the chance. The idea is so strong that it influences his bodily movements—as ideas often do. Thoughts of fear produce "goose-pimples" and sometimes make the blood rush to the hands and feet. God has made us so that, when we are afraid, we should either fight or run.

Our thoughts make our desires, and our desires are the sculptors of our days. The dominant desire is the predominant destiny. Desires are formed in our thoughts and meditations; and since action follows the lead of desires, the soul, as it becomes flooded with divine promptings, becomes less and less a prey to the suggestions of the world. This increases happiness; external wants are never completely satisfied, and their elimination thus makes for less anxiety.

If a man meditates consistently on God, a complete revolution takes place in his behavior. If in a morning meditation he remembers how God became a humble servant of man, he will not lord it over others during the day. If there were a meditation of His redemption of all men, he would cease to be a snob. Since Our Lord took the world's sins upon Himself, the man who has dwelt on this truth will seek to take up the burdens of his neighbor, even though they were not of his making—for the sins the Lord bore were not of His making, either. If the meditation stressed the merciful Savior Who forgave those who crucified Him, so a man will forgive those who injure him, that he may be worthy of forgiveness. These thoughts do not come from ourselves—for we are incapable of them—nor from the world—for they are unworldly thoughts. They come from God alone.

Once our helplessness is rendered up to the power of God, life changes, and we become less and less the victims of our moods. Instead of letting the world determine our state of mind, we determine the state of soul with which the world is to be faced. The earth carries its own atmosphere with it as it revolves about the sun; so the soul can carry the atmosphere of God with it, in disregard of turbulent events in the world outside. There is a moment in every good meditation when the God-life enters our life, and another moment when our life enters the God-life. These events transform us utterly. Sick, nervous, fearful men are made well by this communion of creature with creator, this letting of God into the soul. A distinguished psychiatrist, J. D. Hadfield, has said: "I attempted to cure a nervous patient with suggestions of quiet and confidence, but without success, until I had linked these suggestions on to that faith in the power of God which is the substance of the Christian's confidence and hope. Then the patient became strong."

It is never true to say that we have no time to meditate; the less one thinks of God, the less time there will always be for Him. The time one has for anything depends on how much he values it. Thinking determines the uses of time; time does not rule over thinking. The problem of spirituality is never, then, a question of time; it is a problem of thought. For it does not require much time to make us saints; it requires only much love.

The remedy for the ills that come to us from thinking about time is what might be called the sanctification of the moment—or the "now". Our Lord laid down the rule for us in these words: "Do not fret, then, over tomorrow; leave tomorrow to fret over its own needs; for today, today's troubles are enough" (Mt 6:34). This means that each day has its own trials; we are not to borrow troubles from tomorrow, because that day, too, will have its cross. We are to leave the past to divine mercy and to trust the future, whatever its trials, to His loving providence. Each minute of life has its peculiar duty—regardless of the appearance that minute may take. The now-moment is the moment of salvation. Each complaint against it is a defeat; each act of resignation to it is a victory.

The present moment includes some things over which we have control, but it also carries with it difficulties we cannot avoid—such things as a business failure, a bad cold, rain on picnic days, an unwelcome visitor, a fallen cake, a buzzer that doesn't work, a fly in the milk, and a boil on the nose the night of the dance. We do not always know why such things as sickness and setbacks happen to us, for our minds are far too puny to grasp God's plan.

Man is a little like a mouse in a piano, which cannot understand why it must be disturbed by someone playing Chopin and forcing it to move off the piano wires. When Job suffered, he posed questions to God: Why was he born, and why was he suffering? God appeared to him, but instead of answering Job's questions, He began to ask Job to answer some of the larger questions about the universe. When the Creator had finished pouring into the head of the creature, Job realized that the questions of God were wiser than the answers of men. Because God's ways are not our ways—because the salvation of a soul is more important than all material values—because Divine Wisdom can draw good out of evil—the human mind must develop acceptance of the now, no matter how hard it may be for us to understand its freight of pain. We do not walk out of a theater because the hero is shot in the first act; we give the dramatist credit for having a plot in his mind; so the soul does not walk out on the first act of God's drama of salvation—it is the last act that is to crown the play. The things that happen to us are not always susceptible to our minds' comprehension or wills' conquering; but they are always within the capacity of our faith to accept and of our wills' submission.

Every moment brings us more treasures than we can gather. The great value of the now, spiritually viewed, is that it carries a message God has directed personally to us. Books, sermons, and broadcasts on a religious theme have the appearance of being circular letters, meant for everyone. Sometimes, when such general appeals do appear to have a personal application, the soul gets angry and writes vicious letters to allay its uneasy conscience: excuses can always be found for ignoring the divine law. But though moral and spiritual appeals carry God's identical message to all who listen, this is not true of the now-moment; *no* one else except me is in exactly these circumstances; no one else has to carry the same burden, whether it be sickness, the death of a loved one, or some other adversity. Nothing is more individually tailored to our spiritual needs than the now-moments; for that reason it is an occasion of knowledge which can come to no one else. This moment is my school, my textbook, my lesson. Not even Our Lord disdained to learn from His specific now; being God, He knew all, but there was still one kind of knowledge He could experience as a man. St. Paul describes it: "Son of God though He was, He learned obedience in the school of suffering" (Heb 5:8).

8

Love of God and Resignation to His Will

The love of God has three characteristics. First, it is inexhaustible. Human love can be understood, explained, followed from its source like a mountain stream which can be traced to a spring in the rocks. But divine love is infinite. If we start with the stream—in Holy Communion or in prayer—we soon discover that it runs into the ocean of inexhaustible delights. What we know about love is a minute drop in that ocean. God's love existed before the world began; it will exist after we go; our hearts can hold only its merest particles, as in such loves as Romeo's for Juliet or Dante's for his Beatrice. Love eludes our greatest poets' words, and even the mystics' writings do not capture it.

Second, the love of the Lord is greater in realization than in desire. Here, again, it differs from worldly love, which is greater in anticipation than in realization. All the popular love songs tell us: "How happy we *will* be!" Divine love, on the contrary, does not look at all enchanting or ecstatic before we have it: the Cross frightens us; the sacrifice of selfishness and sin seems like a little death; non-sensual love appears as loneliness. But after one makes the surrender, gives up the field to win the pearl, then one is possessed of a joy that is ineffable, that beggars all

description. The discovery makes one act so differently
that his friends think he has lost his mind; but actually, he
has found his soul, which the believer now would not give
up for anything in all the world.

Third, the love of Our Lord is not affected by suffering. He who loves the Tremendous Lover sometimes
finds, indeed, that pain adds fuel to the flame. Sorrow
remarries the soul to God. St. Thérèse called each trial
that came to her a little present from God. Persons in
adversity taste and find the Lord is sweet. An elderly
woman with arthritis, her limbs twisted like the olive
trees in the Garden of Gethsemane, pours out her oil of
prayers in fifty rosaries a day; a young bride writes in her
diary: "Keep me, O Lord, close to Thy Kingdom that I
may sanctify the flesh and make it the chariot running its
course to the supernal crown of the spirit"; a young husband with an unfaithful wife, but who is consecrated and
dedicated to continence, eats daily of the Bread of Life
so that the bride may one day return to both the home
and the faith; religious women in convents offer prayers
of thanks to God when told they are mortally ill, so that
they may offer their lives as soldiers on the battlefield
of faith in reparation for the evil of the world; soldiers
returning from the battles of a world war enter a religious life that they may now win the battle against the
powers of darkness through a life of silence and penance;
a young woman, heroine of the war, rescuing soldiers,
feeding the diseased, and then contracting their malady
herself, says: "All I want really—*is to love God more*"; a
Jewish psychiatrist [convert] leaves a good practice to
enter one of the strictest orders in the Church to pray for
his own people; a woman in the world promises to fast
from meat and fish for life, in order to bring fallen-away
Catholics back to the embrace of the Master.

Boundless love alone can explain these surrenders! For these are happy people, all of them—it is a joyous thing to live on the divine level. Religion does not seem pleasant to those who have never climbed high enough, by a renunciation of selfishness, to glimpse its vistas; but a divine religion with the Holy Eucharist is much more pleasant to those who experience it than the world is pleasant to those who sin in it. It is possible that a true lover of God may have tasted both worlds, both lives, if he is a convert or a penitent. But the man who has lived only for the flesh, pleasure, and profit has no experience whatever of the thrills of the spirit. Since he has never tasted, he never can compare.

The End of All Human Love Is Doing the Will of God. Even the most frivolous speak of love in terms of eternity. Love is timeless. As true love develops, there are at first two loves facing one another, seeking to possess one another. As love progresses, the two loves, instead of seeking one another, seek an object outside both. They both develop a passion for unity outside themselves, namely, in God. That is why, as a pure Christian love matures, a husband and spouse become more and more religious as time goes on. At first the happiness consisted in doing the will of the other; then the happiness consisted in doing the will of God. True love is a religious act. If I love you as God wills that I love you, it is the highest expression of love.

The last words of Mary that were spoken in Sacred Scripture were the words of total abandonment to the will of God. "Whatsoever He shall say to you, that do ye." As Dante said: "In His will is our peace." Love has no other destiny than to obey Christ. Our wills are ours only to give away. The human heart is torn between a sense of emptiness and a need of being filled, like the waterpots of Cana. The emptiness comes from the fact that we are human. The power of filling belongs only to Him Who ordered the waterpots filled. Lest any heart should fail in being filled, Mary's last valedictory is: "Whatsoever He shall say to you, that do ye." The heart has a need of emptying and a need of being filled. The power of emptying is human—emptying in the love of others—the power of filling belongs only to God. Hence all perfect love must end on the note: "Not my will, but Thine be done, O Lord!"

Obedience does not mean the execution of orders that are given by a drill sergeant. It springs, rather, from the love of an order, and love of Him who gave it. The merit of obedience is less in the act than in the love; the submission, the devotion, and the service which obedience implies are not born of servitude, but are rather effects that spring from and are unified by love. Obedience is servility only to those who have not understood the spontaneity of love.

Our Lord spent three hours in redeeming, three years in teaching, and thirty years in obeying, in order that a rebellious, proud, and diabolically independent world might learn the value of obedience. Home life is the God-appointed training ground of human character, for from the home life of the child springs the maturity of manhood, either for good or for evil. The only recorded acts of Our Blessed Lord's childhood are acts of obedience—to God, His heavenly Father, and also to Mary and Joseph. He thus shows the special duty of childhood and of youth: to obey parents as the vice-regents of God. He, the great God Whom the heavens and earth could not contain, submitted Himself to His parents. If He was sent on a message to a neighbor, it was the great sender of the Apostles Who delivered the message. If Joseph ever bade Him search for a tool that was lost, it was the wisdom of God and the shepherd in search of lost souls Who was actually doing the seeking. If Joseph taught Him carpentry, He Who was taught was One Who had carpentered the universe, and Who would one day be put to death by the members of His own profession. If He made a yoke for the oxen of a neighbor, it was He Who would call Himself a yoke for men—and yet a burden that would be light. If they bade Him work in a little plot of garden ground, to train the creepers or water the flowers, it was He, Who was the great dresser of the vineyard of His Church, Who took in hand the waterpot and the gardening tools. All men may ponder well the hint of a child subject to His parents, that no heavenly call is ever to be trusted which bids one neglect the obvious duties that lie near to hand.

There is an Oriental proverb which says: "The first deities which the child has to acknowledge are his parents." And another says that, "Obedient children are as ambrosia to the gods." The parent is to the child God's representative; and in order that parents may not have a responsibility that will be too heavy for them, God gives each child a soul, as so much clay which their hands can mold in the way of truth and love. Whenever a child is given to parents, a crown is made for it in heaven; and woe to those parents if that child is not reared with a sense of responsibility to acquire that crown!

There are great advantages to an act of resignation to God's will. The first is this: we escape from the power which the "accidents" of life had over us. The accidents of life are those things which interrupt our ordered existence and cancel our plans—mishaps such as a sickness which forces us to defer a trip, or the summons of the telephone when we are tuned in to our favorite program on the radio. It is a medical fact that tense and worried people have more accidents resulting in fractures than those who have a clear conscience and a divine goal in life. Some men and women complain that they "never get a break", that the world is their enemy, that they have "bad luck". A person resigned to God's holy will utters no such complaint; whatever comes along, he welcomes it.

The difference between people who never get the breaks and those who make every now an occasion for thanking God is this: the latter live in an area of love greater than their desire to "have their way". As a waif on the streets suffers misfortunes which the child in a loving family does not know, so the man who has not learned to place full trust in God suffers reverses and disasters which would not appear as troubles to loving souls. God does not show Himself equally to all creatures. He does show all men how to turn everything to joy. This does not mean God is unfair, but only that it is impossible for even Him to show Himself to certain hearts under some conditions. The sunlight has no favorites, but it cannot shine as well on a dusty mirror as on a polished one. In the order of Divinity, there is nothing accidental; there is never a collision of blind forces, hurting us, at random.

It is easy for love to take the beloved for granted and to assume that what was freely offered for life needs no repurchasing. But love can be treated either as an antique that needs no care, or as a flower that needs pruning. Love could become so possessive that it would hardly be conscious of the rights of others: lest love so degenerate into a mutual exchange of egotisms, there must be a constant going out to others, an exteriorization, an increased searching for the formation of an "us". Love of God is inseparable from love of neighbor. Words of love must be translated into action, and they must go beyond the mere boundary of the home. The needs of neighbor may become so imperative that one may have to sacrifice one's own comfort for another. Love that does not expand to neighbor dies of its own too-much.

Mary obeys this third law of love, even in her pregnancy, by visiting a pregnant neighbor, an old woman who is already six months with child. From that day to this, no one who boasts of his love of God may claim exemption from the law to love his neighbor, too. Mary hastens—*Maria festinans*—across the hills to visit her cousin Elizabeth. Mary is present at a birth at this Visitation, as she will later attend a marriage at Cana and a death on Calvary: the three major moments in the life of a neighbor. Now, no sooner does an angel visit her than she makes a visit to a woman in need. A woman is best helped by a woman, and the one woman who bears love divine within her casts such a spell over another woman with child that John the Baptist leaps with joy in her womb. The bearing of Christ is inseparable from the service of Christ. God the Son had come to Mary not for her sake alone, but for the sake of the world. Love is social, or it ceases to be love.

Sanctity is not a question of relinquishing or abandoning or giving up something for Christ; it is a question of exchange. Our Lord never said it was wrong to love the world; He said only that it was a loss, for "what shall a man give in exchange for his soul?" Exchange is founded on the fact that there are two classes of goods. First, things that we can get along without; second, things we cannot get along without. I can very well get along without a dime, but I cannot get along without bread which it will buy, and so, I exchange one for the other. So, too, in the

spiritual world. I soon learn that there are many things
I can get along without, and as I grow in acquaintance
with Christ, I find that I can get along without sin, but I
cannot get along without His peace of conscience, and so
I exchange one for the other. Later on, as I get to know
Him better, I find that I can get along without an innocent
pleasure, but I cannot get along without the pleasure of
daily communion with Him, and so I exchange the one
for the other. I find, by a still deeper acquaintance, that I
can get along without the world's goods, but not without
the wealth of Christ's grace, and so, I exchange one for the
other, and that is the vow of poverty. I find that I can get
along very well without the pleasures of the flesh, but I
cannot get along without the pleasures of Christ's Spirit,
and I exchange the one for the other, and that is the vow
of chastity. I find that I can get along very well without
my own will, but I cannot get along without His, and so
I exchange the one for the other, and that is the vow of
obedience. Thus the saint goes on exchanging one thing
for another. And thus it is that in making himself poor, he
becomes rich, and in making himself a slave, he becomes
free. The gravitation of the earth grows weaker, and the
gravitation of the stars grows stronger, until finally, when
there is nothing left to exchange, like Paul he cries out:
"For me to die is gain", for by that last exchange his gain
is Christ in everlasting life.

Sanctity, then, is not giving up the world. It is exchanging the world. It is a continuation of that sublime
transaction of the Incarnation in which Christ said to
man: "You give Me your humanity, I will give you My
divinity. You give Me your time, I will give you My eternity. You give Me your bonds, I will give you My omnipotence. You give Me your slavery, I will give you My
freedom. You give Me your death, I will give you My life.

You give Me your nothingness, I will give you My all."
And the consoling thought throughout this whole trans-
forming process is that it does not require much time to
make us saints; it requires only much love.

In joy and in sorrow, every heart needs someone who will
suspend his own preoccupations to listen to its own artic-
ulation, needs someone who will drop all his cares to take
on the burden of its own. The most unfortunate mortals
are those who shed their tears in silence and find no one to
wipe those tears away. How many men and women there
are in the world who, through sin, have felt themselves
alone, cast off from everyone, who in their inmost heart
have felt the need of some sanctuary into which they might
retire for consolation and direction. Our cities are full of
souls who are constantly crying out, "What can I do?" and
to these and the millions who are craving for someone
who will understand and pardon, as Christ understood and
pardoned weak Peter and sensuous Magdalen, the confessional is the answer.

Furthermore, in defense of the penitent's side of the
case, does not experience reveal and history tell us that an
honest avowal of our guilt has a certain reparative value?
All mankind has recognized in a spontaneous confession
the quality of expiation and the merit of pardon. Only
one sentiment dominates this point—from the mother
who interrogates her child in an attempt to make the
child openly avow its faults by saying, "Tell me and I will
not punish you"; up to the honor systems in our colleges
under which young men are told to be men enough to
"stand up" and acknowledge their guilt; on finally to the
judge who interrogates from his bench the criminal—and
that sentiment is one which tempers the punishment when
a man pleads guilty.

Now, if a man himself accords pardon on the ground of repentance by humbly avowing his fault, why should not God do the same on similar conditions? That is precisely what Our Blessed Lord has done. He has taken the natural avowal which has an expiatory force and elevated it to the dignity of a sacrament. An avowal is human but He has divinized it. What is natural He has made supernatural. That which has always been the indispensable condition for granting pardon, namely, the open avowal of guilt, is the condition upon which Almighty God has granted His pardon in the sacrament of mercy. And so with that infinite tenderness of Him, He told the story of the Prodigal Son who came back to his father, acknowledged his guilt, and was rewarded with the embrace and kiss of his father. Such is the joy of God on sinners returning, for "even so there shall be joy in heaven upon one sinner that doth penance, more than upon ninety-nine just who need not penance."

Saints have a sense of humor. I do not mean only canonized saints, but rather that great army of staunch and solid Christians to whom everything and every incident speaks a story of God's love. A saint can be defined as one who has a divine sense of humor, for a saint never takes this world seriously as the lasting city. To him the world is like a scaffolding up through which souls climb to the Kingdom of heaven, and when the last soul shall have climbed up through it, then it shall be torn down and burned with a fervent fire, not because it is base, but simply because it has done its work—it has brought souls back again to God. A saint is one who looks out upon this world as a nursery to the Father's heavenly mansion and a steppingstone to the Kingdom of heaven. A saint is one to whom everything in the world is a sacrament. In the strict sense of the terms, there are only seven sacraments, but in the broad sense of the term everything in the world is a sacrament, for everything in the world can be used as a means of special sanctification. A saint is one who never complains about the particular duty of his state in life, for he knows full well that "all the world's a stage, and all the men and women merely players." Why, then, should he who plays the part of a king glory in his tinsel crown and tin sword, and believe that he is better than someone else who plays the part of a peasant, for when the curtain goes down they are all men? So, too, why should anyone, who in this world happens to enjoy either the accident of honor or wealth, believe he is better than someone else who may possess neither gold nor worldly learning? Why should he glory in his tinseled crown and tin sword, and believe that he is better than someone else who plays a less important role in the great drama of life? For when the curtain goes down on the Last Day, and we respond to the curtain call of judgment, we will not be asked what part we played, but how well we played the part that was assigned to us.

A saint, then, is one who has learned to spiritualize and sacramentalize and ennoble everything in the world, and make of it a prayer. No occupation is too base for such spiritualization, nor is any suffering too hard for ennobling. It is only those who have not this highly developed sense that let the opportunities of daily life pass by without either making of them a prayer, or drawing from them a divine lesson. Centuries ago, according to a story perhaps apocryphal, in the streets of Florence there stood a beautiful piece of Carrara marble that had been cut and hacked and ruined by some cheap artist. Other mediocre artists passed it by, and bemoaned that it should have been so ruined. One day Michelangelo passed it and asked that it be brought to his studio. He there applied to it his chisel, his genius, and his inspiration. He drew out of it the immortal statue of David. The lesson contained herein is that there is nothing so base or low that it cannot be reconquered, that there is no duty however menial that cannot be retrieved for sanctity, and that there is nothing that is cast down that cannot be lifted up.

Down in the gutter of a city street was a drop of water, soiled, dirty, and stagnant. Way up in the heavens a gentle sunbeam saw it, leaped out of its azure sky, down to the drop, kissed it, thrilled it through and through with new strange life and hope, and lifted it up higher and higher and higher, beyond the clouds, and one day let it fall as a flake of immaculate snow on a mountain-top. And so our own lives—humdrum, routine, tiresome lives of a workaday world—can be ennobled, spiritualized, and sacramentalized, provided we bring to them the inspiration of Someone who saw apostolic zeal in salt, provided we infuse their carbon blackness with the electric flame of love which will make them glow with the brilliance of a diamond, provided we bring to them the inspiration of the great captain who carries five wounds in the forefront of battle, and thrills them with the fixed flash of the lightning made eternal as the light.

And when we have done this, then perhaps we will understand why He Who came to this earth to teach us the divine sense of humor showed us everything that was lovely and beautiful in His character—except one thing. He showed us His power; He showed us His wisdom; He showed us His melting kindness; He showed us His forgiveness; He showed us His power over nature; He showed us His knowledge of human hearts; but there was one thing that He did not show; there was one thing He saved for those who do not take this world too seriously;

there was one thing He saved for paradise; there was one thing He saved for those who, like poets and saints, have a divine sense of humor; there was one thing He saved for heaven that will make heaven heaven, and that was— His smile!

Everything that happens has been foreseen and known by God from all eternity, and is either willed by Him, or at least permitted.

God's knowledge does not grow as ours does, from ignorance to wisdom. The Fall did not catch God napping. God is science, but He is not a scientist. God knows all, but He learns nothing from experience. He does not look down on you from heaven as you look down on an anthill, seeing you going in and out of your house, walking to work, and then telling an angel-secretary to record the unkind word you said to the grocer boy.

Why is it we always think of God as watching the bad things we do, and never the good deeds? God does not keep a record of your deeds. You do your own bookkeeping. Your conscience takes your own dictation. God knows all things merely by looking into Himself, not by reading over your shoulder.

An architect can tell you how many rooms will be in your house, and the exact size of each, before the house is built because he is the cause of the becoming of that house. God is the cause of the *being* of all things. He knows all before they happen.

As a motion picture reel contains the whole story before it is thrown upon the screen, so God knows all. But before it is acted on the stage of history, God knows all the possible radii that can be drawn from a point in the center to the circumference. He, therefore, knows all the possible directions your human will can take.

Do not think that because God knows all that, therefore He has predetermined you to heaven and hell independently of your merits and irrespective of your freedom. Remember that in God there is no future. God knows all, not in the succession of time, but in the "now standing still" of eternity, i.e., all at once. His knowledge that you shall act in a particular manner is not the immediate cause of your acting, any more than your knowledge that you are sitting down caused you to sit down, or prevents you from getting up, if you willed to do it.

Our Blessed Mother could have refused the dignity of becoming the Mother of God, as Judas could have resisted the temptation to betray or could have repented. The fact that God knew what each would do did not make them act the way they did. Since you are free, you can act contrary to God's will. If a doctor knows that it is all for your good to undergo an operation, you must not blame him, if you refuse to have the operation and lose your health. Free will either cooperates with or rebels against predestination; it does not "surmount" it.

Because there is no future in God, foreknowing is not forecausing. You may know the stock market very well, and in virtue of your superior wisdom foretell that such and such a stock will sell for fifty points in three months. In three months it does reach fifty points. Did you *cause* it to reach fifty points, or did you foreknow it?

You may be in a tower where you can see, advancing in the distance, a man who has never been over that terrain before. You know that before he reaches the tower he must cross that ditch, wade that pond, tramp those bushes, and climb that hill. You foresee all the possibilities, but you do not cause him to cross those obstacles. The pilot is free to drive his ship, but he is not free to drive the waves.

While God has given to each of us the power to act, He has left us free to exercise the power. Why then blame

God when we abuse our freedom? God will not destroy your freedom. Hell is the eternal guarantee of our freedom to rebel, or of the power to make fools out of ourselves.

The following story illustrates the fallacy of predestination without freedom: In the Colonial days of our country, there was a wife who believed in a peculiar kind of predestination which left no room for human freedom. Her husband, who did not share her eccentricities, one day left for the market. He came back after a few minutes saying he forgot his gun. She said: "You are either predestined to be shot, or you are not predestined to be shot. If you are predestined to be shot, the gun will do you no good. If you are not predestined to be shot, you will not need it. Therefore, do not take your gun."

But he answered: "Suppose I am predestined to be shot by an Indian on condition I do not have my gun?" That was sound religion. It allowed for human freedom. We are our own creators. To those who ask: "If God knew I would lose my soul, why did He make me?" The answer is: "God did not make you as a lost soul. You made yourself." The universe is moral and, therefore, conditional: "Behold I stand at the door and knock!" God knocks! He breaks down no doors. The latch is on our side, not God's.

God permits evil things for the reason of a greater good related to His love and the salvation of our souls.

God does permit evil. In the strong language of Scripture: "He that spared not even his own Son; but delivered Him up for us all" (Rom 8:32). Our Lord told Judas: "This is your hour" (Lk 22:53). Evil does have its hour. All that it can do within that hour is to put out the lights of the world. But God has His day.

The evil of the world is inseparable from human freedom, and hence the cost of destroying the world's evil would be the destruction of human freedom. Certainly none of us want to pay that high a price, particularly since

God would never permit evil unless He could draw some good from it.

God can draw good out of evil because, while the power of doing evil is ours, the effects of our evil deeds are outside our control, and, therefore, in the hands of God. You are free to break the law of gravitation, but you have no control over the effects of throwing yourself from the top of the Washington Monument.

The brethren of Joseph were free to toss him into a well, but from that point on Joseph was in God's hands. Rightly did he say to his brethren: "You intended it for evil, but God for good." The executioners were free to nail Our Lord to the cross, Judas was free to betray, the judges were free to misjudge, but they could not prevent the effect of their evil deed, viz., the Crucifixion, being used by God as the means of our redemption.

St. Peter spoke of it as an evil deed, as known and permitted by God. "Jesus of Nazareth, a man approved of God among you, by miracles, and wonders, and signs, which God did by him, in the midst of you, as you also know: The same being delivered up, by the determinate counsel and foreknowledge of God, you by the hands of wicked men have crucified and slain. Whom God hath raised up, having loosed the sorrows of hell, as it was impossible that he should be holden by it" (Acts 2:22–24).

The evil which God permits must not be judged by its immediate effects, but rather by its ultimate effects. When you go to a theater, you do not walk out because you see a good man suffering in the first act. You give the dramatist credit for a plot. Why can you not do that much with God?

The mouse in the piano cannot understand why anyone should disturb his gnawing at the keys by making weird sounds. Much less can our puny minds grasp the plan of God. Martha could not understand why Lazarus should die, particularly because Lazarus was the friend of Our Lord. But Our Lord told her it was in order that God's power might be revealed in the resurrection from the death. The slaughter of the Innocents probably saved many boys from growing up into men who on Good Friday would have shouted "Crucify!"

We must do everything within our power to fulfill God's will as it is made known to us by His Mystical Body, the Commandments and our lawfully constituted superiors, and the duties flowing from our state in life. Everything that is outside our power, we must abandon and surrender to His Holy Will.

Notice the distinction between *within our power*, and *outside our power*. There is to be no fatalism. Some things are under our control. We are not to be like the man who perilously walked the railing of a ship in a storm at sea saying: "I am a fatalist! I believe that when your time comes, there is nothing you can do about it." There was much more wisdom in the preacher who said: "You run up against a brick wall every now and then during life. If God wants you to go through that wall, it is up to God to make the hole."

We are here concerned with those things outside your power, e.g., sickness, accident, bumps on buses, trampled toes in subways, the barbed word of a fellow worker; rain on picnic days, the death of Aunt Ellen on your wedding day, colds on vacation, the loss of your purse, and moth balls in your suit.

God could have prevented any of these things. He could have stopped your headache, prevented a bullet from hitting your boy, forestalled cramps during a swim, and killed the germ that laid you low. If He did not, it was for a superior reason. Therefore, say: "God's will be done."

If you tell a citizen of Erin it is a bad day, nine times out of ten he will answer: "It's a good day to save your soul." Maybe there is no such thing in God's eyes as bad weather; perhaps there are only good clothes. We must not think that God is good because we have a fat bank account. Providence is not the Provident Loan. Sanctity consists in accepting whatever happens to us as God's will, and even thanking Him for it. "Not every one that saith to me, Lord, Lord, shall enter into the kingdom of heaven: but he that doth the will of my Father Who is in heaven, he shall enter into the kingdom of heaven" (Mt 7:21).

Do not become impatient with God because He does not answer your prayers immediately. We are always in a hurry; God is not. Perhaps that is one of the reasons why so few Americans like Rome: they heard it was not built in a day. Evil things are generally done quickly. "What thou dost, do quickly" (Jn 13:27).

In a certain sense there is no unanswered prayer. Is there a father in the world who ever refused the request of his son for a gift which would not be good for him, who did not pick him up and give him a sign of love that made him forget the request?

Every moment comes to you pregnant with a divine purpose; time being so precious that God deals it out only second by second. Once it leaves your hands and your power to do with it as you please, it plunges into eternity, to remain forever whatever you made it.

Does not the scientist gain more control over nature by humbly sitting down before the facts of nature and being docile to its teachings? In like manner, surrender yourself to God, and all is yours. It is one of the paradoxes of creation that we gain control by submission. You will thus learn to appreciate the advantages of disadvantages.

Your very handicaps will not be reasons for despair, but points of departure for new horizons. When caught within circumstances beyond your control, make them creative of peace by surrender to the divine will. From prison St. Paul wrote: "Be mindful of my bands. Grace be with you" (Col 4:18). Others would have said: "I am in prison. God give me grace."

Circumstances must not control you; you must control circumstances. *Do* something to them! Even the irritations of life can be made stepping stones to salvation. An oyster develops a pearl because a grain of sand irritated it. Cease talking about your pains and aches. Thank God for them: an act of thanksgiving when things go against our will, then a thousand acts of thanksgiving when things go according to our will.

"Giving thanks always for all things in the name of Our Lord Jesus Christ, to God and Father" (Eph 5:20). God does not will the sin of those who hate you, but He does will your humiliation. Things happen against your will but nothing, except sin, happens against God's will. When the messenger came to Job saying that the Sabeans had stolen his livestock and killed his sons, Job did not say: "The Lord gave me wealth; the Sabeans took it away." He did say: "The Lord gave, and the Lord hath taken away: as it hath pleased the Lord so is it done: blessed be the name of the Lord" (Job 1:21).

When anyone asks you, "How are you?" remember it is not a question, but a greeting!

If you trust in God and surrender to His will, you are always happy, for "to them that love God, all things work together unto good" (Rom 8:28). "Whatsoever shall befall the just man, it shall not make him sad" (Prov 12:21).

Discouragement is a form of pride; sadness is often caused by our egotism. If you will whatever God wills, you always have exactly what you want. When you want anything else, you are not happy before you get it, and when you do get it, you do not want it. That is why you are "up" today and "down" tomorrow.

You will never be happy if your happiness depends on getting solely what you want. Change the focus. Get a new center. Will what God wills, and your joy no man shall take from you. "So also you now indeed have sorrow; but I will see you again, and your heart shall rejoice; and your joy no man shall take from you. And in that day you shall not ask me anything. Amen, amen I say to you: if you ask the Father any thing in my name, he will give it you. Hitherto you have not asked any thing in my name. Ask, and you shall receive; that your joy may be full" (Jn 16:22–24).

Be not afraid, "For this is the will of God, your sanctification" (1 Thess 4:3). Think not that you could do more good if you were well, or that you could be more kind if you had more money, or that you could exercise more power for good if you had another position! What matters is not what we are, or what we are doing, but whether we are doing God's will!

Place not your trust in God because of your merits! He loves you despite your unworthiness. It is His love which will make you better rather than your betterment which will make Him love you. Often during the day say: "God loves me, and He is on my side, by my side."

Believe firmly that God's action toward you is a masterpiece of partiality and love. Be not like a child who wants to help his father fix the car before he is trained to do it! Give God a chance to love you, to show His will, to train you in His affection. Rejoice! I say again, rejoice: "Thy will be done on earth as it is in heaven."

9

The Role of Mary in the Church

One cannot go to a statue of a mother holding a babe, hack away the mother, and expect to have the babe. Touch her and you spoil Him. All other world religions are lost in myth and legend except Christianity. Christ is cut off from all the gods of paganism because He is tied to woman and to history: "Born of the Virgin Mary; suffered under Pontius Pilate". Coventry Patmore rightly calls Mary: "Our only savior from an abstract Christ." It is easier to understand the meek and humble heart of Christ by looking at His Mother. She holds all the great truths of Christianity together, as a piece of wood holds a kite. Children wrap the string of a kite around a stick, and release the string as the kite climbs to the heavens. Mary is like that piece of wood. Around her we wrap all the precious strings of the great truths of our holy faith—for example, the Incarnation, the Eucharist, the Church. No matter how far we get above the earth, as the kite may, we always have need of Mary to hold the doctrines of the Creed together. If we threw away the stick, we would no longer have the kite; if we threw away Mary, we would never have Our Lord. He would be lost in the heavens, like our runaway kite, and that would be terrible, indeed, for us on earth.

Mary does not prevent our honoring Our Lord. Nothing is more cruel than to say that she takes souls away from

Christ. That could mean that Our Lord chose a mother who is selfish, He Who is love Itself. If she kept us from her Son, we would disown her! But is not she, who is the Mother of Jesus, good enough for us sinners? We would never have had Our Divine Lord if He had not chosen her.

We pray to the heavenly Father, "Give us this day our daily bread." Though we ask *God* for our daily bread, we do not hate the farmer or the baker who help prepare it. Neither does the mother who gives the bread to her child dispense with the heavenly provider. If the only charge Our Lord has against us on Judgment Day is that we loved His Mother—then we shall be very happy!

As our love does not start with Mary, so neither does it stop with Mary. Mary is a window through which our humanity first catches a glimpse of divinity on earth. Or perhaps she is more like a magnifying glass, that intensifies our love of her Son, and makes our prayers more bright and burning.

God, Who made the sun, also made the moon. The moon does not take away from the brilliance of the sun. The moon would be only a burnt-out cinder floating in the immensity of space, were it not for the sun. All its light is reflected from the sun. The Blessed Mother reflects her Divine Son; without Him, she is nothing. With Him, she is the mother of men. On dark nights we are grateful for the moon; when we see it shining, we know there must be a sun. So in this dark night of the world when men turn their backs on Him Who is the light of the world, we look to Mary to guide their feet while we await the sunrise.

Every person carries within his heart a blueprint of the one he loves. What seems to be "love at first sight" is actually the fulfillment of desire, the realization of a dream. Plato, sensing this, said that all knowledge is a recollection from a previous existence. This is not true, as he states it, but it *is* true if one understands it to mean that we already have an ideal in us, one which is made by our thinking, our habits, our experiences, and our desires. Otherwise, how would we know immediately, on seeing persons or things, that we loved them? Before meeting certain people we already have a pattern and mold of what we like and what we do not like; certain persons fit into that pattern, others do not.

When we hear music for the first time, we either like or dislike it. We judge it by the music we already have heard in our own hearts. Jittery minds, which cannot long repose in one object of thought or in continuity of an ideal, love music which is distracting, excited, and jittery. Calm minds like calm music: the heart has its own secret melody and one day, when the score is played, the heart answers: "This is it." So it is with love. A tiny architect works inside the human heart drawing sketches of the ideal love from the people it sees, from the books it reads, from its hopes and daydreams, in the fond hope that the eye may one day see the ideal and the hand touch it. Life becomes satisfying the moment the dream is seen walking, and the person appears as the incarnation of all that one loved. The liking is instantaneous—because, actually, it was there waiting for a long time. Some go through life without ever meeting *what they call* their ideal. This could be very disappointing, if the ideal never really existed. But the absolute ideal of every heart does exist, and it is God. All human love is an initiation into the eternal. Some find the ideal in substance without passing through the shadow.

God, too, has within Himself blueprints of everything in the universe. As the architect has in his mind a plan of the house before the house is built, so God has in His mind an archetypal idea of every flower, bird, tree, springtime, and melody. There never was a brush touched to canvas nor a chisel to marble without some great pre-existing idea. So, too, every atom and every rose is a realization and concretion of an idea existing in the mind of God from all eternity. All creatures below man correspond to the pattern God has in His mind. A tree is truly a tree because it corresponds to God's idea of a tree. A rose is a rose because it is God's idea of a rose wrapped up in chemicals and tints and life. *But it is not so with persons.* God has to have two pictures of us: one is what we are, and the other is what we *ought to be.* He has the *model,* and He has the reality: the blueprint and the edifice, the score of the music and the way we play it. God has to have these two pictures because in each and every one of us there is some disproportion and want of conformity between the original plan and the way we have worked it out. The image is blurred; the print is faded. For one thing, our personality is not complete in time; we need a renewed body. Then, too, our sins diminish our personality; our evil acts daub the canvas the master hand designed. Like unhatched eggs, some of us refuse to be warmed by the divine love which is so necessary for incubation to a higher level. We are in constant need of repairs; our free acts do not coincide with the law of our being; we fall short of all God wants us to be. St. Paul tells us that we were predestined, before the foundations of the world were laid, to become the sons of God. But some of us will not fulfill that hope.

There is, actually, only one person in all humanity of whom God has one picture, and in whom there is a perfect conformity between what He wanted her to be and what she is, and that is His own Mother. Most of us are a minus sign, in the sense that we do not fulfill the high hopes the heavenly Father has for us. But Mary is the equal sign. The ideal that God had of her, that she *is,* and in the flesh. The model and the copy are perfect; she is all that was foreseen, planned, and dreamed. The melody of her life is played just as it was written. Mary was thought, conceived, and planned as the equal sign between ideal and history, thought and reality, hope and realization.

That is why, through the centuries, Christian liturgy has applied to her the words of the Book of Proverbs. Because she is what God wanted us all to be, she speaks of herself as the eternal blueprint in the mind of God, the one whom God loved before she was a creature. She is even pictured as being with Him not only at creation, but before creation. She existed in the divine mind as an eternal thought before there were any mothers. She is the Mother of Mothers—*She is the world's first love.*

A woman elevates man because woman finds less repose in mediocrity than man. The more a person is attached to the practical, the concrete, the monetary, and the material, the more his soul becomes indifferent to great values and, in particular, to the Tremendous Lover. Nothing so dulls the soul as counting, and only what is material can be counted. The woman is more idealistic, less content over a long period of time with the material, and more quickly disillusioned about the carnal. She is more *amphibious* than man, in the sense that she moves with great facility in the two zones of matter and spirit.

The oft-repeated suggestion that woman is more religious than man has some basis in truth, but only in the sense that her nature is more readily disposed toward the ideal. The woman has a greater measure of the eternal and man a greater measure of time, but both are essential for an incarnational universe, in which eternity embraces time in a stable of Bethlehem. When there is descent into an equal degree of vice, there is always a greater scandal caused by a woman than the man. Nothing seems more a profanation of the sacred than a drunken woman. The so-called "double standard", which does not exist and which has no ethical foundation, is actually based on the unconscious impulse of man to regard woman as the preserver of ideals, even when he fails to live up to them.

Woman stands up better in a crisis than man. The best way to arrive at a conclusion is to go to the greatest crisis the world ever faced, namely, the Crucifixion of Our Divine Lord. When we come to this great drama of Calvary, there is one fact that stands out very clearly: *men failed*. Judas, who had eaten at His table, lifted up his heel against Him, sold Him for thirty pieces of silver, and then blistered His lips with a kiss, suggesting that all betrayals of divinity are so terrible that they must be prefaced by some mark of esteem and affection. Pilate, the typical time-serving politician, afraid of incurring the hatred of his government if he released a man whom he already admitted was innocent, sentenced Him to death. Annas and Caiaphas resorted to illegal night trials and false witnesses, and rent their garments as if scandalized at His divinity. The three chosen Apostles, who had witnessed the Transfiguration and, therefore, were thought strong enough to endure the scandal of seeing the shepherd struck, slept in a moment of greatest need, because they were unworried and untroubled. On the way to Calvary, a stranger, interested only in the drama of a man going to execution, was compelled to offer Him a helping hand. On Calvary itself, there is only one of the twelve Apostles present, John, and one wonders if even he would have been there had it not been for the presence of the Mother of Jesus.

On the other hand, there is not a single instance of a woman's failing Him. At the trial, the only voice that is raised in His defense is the voice of a woman. Braving the fury of court officials, she breaks into the judgment hall and bids her husband, Pilate, not to condemn the "just man". On the way to Calvary, although a man is forced to help carry the cross, the pious women of Jerusalem, ignoring the mockery of the soldiers and bystanders, console Him with words of sympathy. One of them wipes His face with a towel, and, forever after, has the name Veronica, which means "true image", for it was His image the Savior left on her towel. On Calvary itself, there are three women present, and the name of each is Mary: Mary of Magdala, who is forever at His feet, and will be there again on Easter morn; Mary of Cleophas, the mother of James and John; and Mary, the Mother of Jesus—the three types of souls forever to be found beneath the Cross of Christ: penitence, motherhood, and virginity.

Since woman today has failed to restrain man, we must look to *The Woman* to restore purity. The Church proclaims two dogmas of purity for The Woman: one, the purity of soul in the Immaculate Conception, the other, the purity of body in the Assumption. Purity is not glorified as ignorance; for when the Virgin Birth was announced to Mary, she said, "I know not man." This meant not only that she was untaught by pleasures; it also implied that she had so brought her soul to focus on inwardness that she was a virgin, not only through the *absence of man*, but through the *Presence of God*. No greater inspiration to purity has the world ever known than The Woman, whose own life was so pure that God chose her as His Mother. But she also understands human frailty and so is prepared to lift souls out of the mire into peace, as at the Cross she chose as her companion the converted sinner Magdalen. Through all the centuries, to those who marry to be loved, Mary teaches that they should marry to love. To the unwed, she bids them all keep the secret of purity until an annunciation, when God will send them a partner; to those who, in carnal love, allow the body to swallow the soul, she bids that the soul envelop the body. To the twentieth century, with its Freud and sex, she bids man to be made again to the God-like image through herself as The Woman while she, in turn, with "traitorous trueness and loyal deceits" betrays us to Christ—Who in His turn delivers us to the Father, that God may be all in all.

10

Suffering and Consolation

The world is full of those who suffer unjustly and who through no fault of their own bear the "slings and arrows of outrageous fortune". What should be our attitude to those who speak untruly of us, who malign our good names, who steal our reputations, and who sneer at our acts of kindness?

The answer is to be found in the First Word from the Cross: *forgive*. If there was ever anyone who had a right to protest against injustice it was He Who is divine justice; if ever there was anyone who was entitled to reproach those who dug His hands and feet with steel, it was Our Lord on the Cross.

And yet, at that very moment when a tree turns against Him and becomes a cross, when iron turns against Him and becomes nails, when roses turn against Him and become thorns, when men turn against Him and become executioners, He lets fall from His lips for the first time in the history of the world a prayer for enemies: "Father, forgive them, for they know not what they do" (Lk 23:34).

Dwell for a moment on what He did not say. He did not say: "I am innocent", and yet who else could have better claimed innocence? Many times before this Good Friday and many times since, men have been sent to a cross, a guillotine, or a scaffold, for a crime they never committed; but not one of them has ever failed to cry: "I am innocent."

But Our Lord made no such protest, for it would have been to have assumed falsely that man is the judge of God. Now if Our Lord, Who was innocence, refrained from asserting His innocence, then we who are not without sin should not forever be crying our innocence.

To do this is wrongly to admit that man, and not God, is our judge. Our souls are to be judged not before the tribunal of men, but before the throne of the God of love; and He "who sees in secret will reward in secret". Our eternal salvation does not depend on how the world judges us, but on how God judges us.

It matters little if our fellow citizens condemn us even when we are right, for truth always finds its contradictors; that is why truth is now nailed to a Cross. What does matter is that we be found right in God's judgment, for in that our eternal happiness depends. There is every chance in the world that the two judgments will differ, for man sees only the face, but God reads the heart. We can fool men, but we cannot fool God.

There was another thing Our Blessed Lord did not say to the representatives of Caesar and the Temple who sent Him to the Cross, namely, "You are unjust." The Father gave all judgment unto Him and yet He does not judge man and say: "You will suffer for this." He knew, being God as well as man, that while there is life there is hope, and His patient suffering before death might purchase the souls of many who now condemn.

Why judge them before the time for judgment? Longinus of the Roman army and Joseph of the Sanhedrin would come to His saving embrace and forgiveness even before He was taken down from the cross. The sinner of this hour might be the saint of the next.

One reason for a long life is penance. Time is given us not just to accumulate that which we cannot take with us, but to make reparation for our sins.

That is why in the parable of the fig tree which had not borne fruit for three years and which the owner wished to cut down because it "cumbereth the ground" the dresser of the vineyard said: "... Let it alone this year also, until I dig about it, and dung it. And if happily it bear fruit ..." (Lk 13:6–9).

So the Lord is with the wicked. He gives them another month, another year of life that they may dig their soul with penance and dung it with mortification, and happily save their souls.

If then the Lord did not judge His executioners before the hour of their judgment, why should we, who really know nothing about them anyway, judge them even when they do us wrong? While they live, may not our refraining from judgment be the very means of their conversion? In any case, judgment has not been given to us, and the world may be thankful that it has not, for God is a more merciful judge than man. "Judge not that you may not be judged" (Mt 7:1).

What Our Lord did say on the Cross was, *forgive*. Forgive your Pilates, who are too weak to defend your justice; forgive your Herods, who are too sensual to perceive your spirituality; forgive your Judases, who think worth is to be measured in terms of silver. "Forgive them—for they know not what they do."

In that sentence is packed the united love of Father and Son, whereby the holy love of God met the sin of man, and remained innocent. This First Word of forgiveness is the strongest evidence of Our Lord's absolute sinlessness. The rest of us at our death must witness the great parade of our sins, and the sight of them is so awful that we dare not go before God without a prayer for pardon.

Yet Jesus, on dying, craved no forgiveness, for He had no sin. The forgiveness He asked was for those who accused Him of sin. And the reason He asked for pardon was that "they know not what they do."

He is God as well as man, which means He knows all the secrets of every human heart. Because He knows all, He can find an excuse: "they know not what they do." But we know so little of our enemies' hearts and so little of the circumstances of their acts and the good faith mingled with their evil deeds, that we are less likely to find an excuse. Because we are ignorant of their hearts, we are apt to be less excusing.

In order to judge others we must be inside them and outside them, but only God can do this. Our neighbors are just as impenetrable to us as we are to them. Judgment on our part, then, would be wrong, for to judge without a mandate is unjust. Our Lord alone has a mandate to judge; we have not.

If possessing that mandate, and knowing all, He still found reason to forgive, then we who have no jurisdiction and who cannot possibly with our puny minds know our neighbors' hearts, have only one thing left to do; that is, to pray: "Father, forgive ... for they know not what they do."

Our Lord used the word "forgive", because He was innocent and knew all, but we must use it for other reasons. First because we have been forgiven greater sins by God. Second because only by forgiving can hate be banished from the world. And third because our own pardon is conditioned by the pardon we extend to others.

Firstly, we must forgive others because God has forgiven us. There is no injustice any person has ever committed against us which is comparable to the injustice we commit against God by our sins. It is this idea Our Lord suggests in the parable of the unmerciful servant (Mt 18:21–35) who was forgiven a debt of ten thousand talents by his master, and immediately afterward went out and choked a fellow servant who owed him only a hundred pence.

The debt which the master forgave the servant was 1,250,000 times greater than the debt owed by the fellow servant. In this great disproportion is revealed how much greater are man's sins against God than are the sins of our fellow men against us. We must therefore forgive our enemies, because we have been forgiven the greater sin of treating God as an enemy.

And if we do not forgive the sins of our enemies, it is very likely because we have never cast up our accounts with God. Herein is to be found the secret of so much of the violence and bitterness of some men in our modern world; they refuse to think of themselves as ever having offended God and therefore never think of themselves as needing pardon.

They think they need no pardon, hence no one else should ever have it. The man who knows not his own guilt before God is apt to be most unforgiving to others, as David at the time of his worst sin.

Our condemnation is often the veil for our own weakness; we cover up our own nakedness with the mantle of criticism; we see the mote in our brother's eye, but never the beam in our own. We carry all our neighbor's faults on a sack in front of us, and all our own on a sack behind us.

The cruelest master is the man who never learned to obey, and the severest judge is the man who never examines his own conscience. The man who is conscious of his need of absolution is the one who is most likely to be indulgent to others.

Such was Paul, who, writing to Titus, finds a reason for being merciful to men: "For we ourselves also were some time unwise, incredulous, erring, slaves to divers desires and pleasures, living in malice and envy, hateful, and hating one another" (Tit 3:3).

It is the forgetfulness of its own sins which makes modern hate so deep and bitter. Men throttle their neighbor for a penny because they forget God forgave them a debt of ten thousand talents. Let them only think of how good God has been to them, and they will begin to be good to others.

A second reason for forgiving those who make us suffer unjustly is that if we do not forgive, hate will multiply until the whole world is hateful. Hate is extremely fertile; it reproduces itself with amazing rapidity.

Communism knows hate can disrupt society more quickly than armies can; that is why it never speaks of charity. That too is why it sows hatred in labor against capital; hatred in atheists against religion; hatred in itself against all who oppose it.

How can all this hatred be stopped when one man is slapping another on the cheek? There is only one way, and that is by turning the other cheek, which means: "I forgive; I refuse to hate you. If I hate you, I will add my quota to the sum total of hate. This I refuse to do. I will kill your hate, I will drive it from the earth. I will love you."

That was the way Stephen conquered the hate of those who killed him; namely, by praying: "Lord, lay not this sin to their charge" (Acts 7:60). He was practically repeating the First Word from the Cross.

And that prayer of forgiveness won over the heart of a young man named Saul who stood nearby, holding the garments of those who stoned him, and "consenting to his death". If Stephen had cursed Saul, Saul might never have become St. Paul. What a loss that would have been! But hate lost the day because Stephen forgave.

Finally we must forgive others for on no other condition will our own sins be forgiven. In fact, it is almost a moral impossibility for God to forgive us unless we in turn forgive. Has He not said: "Blessed are the merciful: for they shall obtain mercy" (Mt 5:7). "Forgive, and you shall be forgiven. Give, and it shall be given unto you ... For with the same measure that you shall mete withal, it shall be measured to you again" (Lk 6:37, 38).

The law is inescapable. Unless we sow, we shall not reap; unless we show mercy to our fellow men, God will revoke His mercy toward us. As in the parable the master canceled the forgiveness of the servant because he refused to show a smaller mercy to his fellow man, "so also shall my heavenly Father do to you, if you forgive not every one his brother from your hearts" (Mt 18:35).

If a box is filled with salt it cannot be filled with sand, and if our hearts are filled with hatred of our neighbor, how can God fill them with His love? It is just as simple as that. There can be and there will be no mercy toward us unless we ourselves are merciful. The real test of the Christian then is not how much he loves his friends, but how much he loves his enemies.

The divine command is clear: "Love your enemies; do good to them that hate you, and pray for them that persecute and calumniate you, that you may be the children of your Father who is in heaven, who maketh his sun to rise upon the good, and bad, and raineth upon the just and the unjust.

"For if you love them that love you, what reward shall you have? do not even the publicans this? And if you salute your brethren only, what do you more? do not also the heathens this?" (Mt 5:44–47).

Forgive then! Forgive even seventy times seven! Soften the pillow of death by forgiving your enemies their little sins against you, that you may be forgiven your great sins against God. Forgive those who hate you, that you may conquer them by love. Forgive those who injure you, that you may be forgiven your offenses.

The First Word from the Cross tells us what should be our attitude toward unjust suffering, but the Second Word tells us what should be our attitude toward pain. There are two ways of looking at it; one is to see it without purpose, the other to see it with purpose.

The first view regards pain as opaque, like a stone wall; the other view regards it as transparent, like a window pane. The way we will react to pain depends entirely upon our philosophy of life. As the poet has put it:

> Two men looked out through their prison bars;
> The one saw mud, the other stars.

In like manner, there are those who, looking upon a rose, would say: "Isn't it a pity that those roses have thorns"; while others would say: "Isn't it consoling that those thorns have roses." These two attitudes are manifested in the two thieves crucified on either side of Our Blessed Lord. The thief on the right is the model for those for whom pain has a meaning; the thief on the left is the symbol of unconsecrated suffering.

Consider first the thief on the left. He suffered no more than the thief on the right, but he began and ended his crucifixion with a curse. Never for a moment did he correlate his sufferings with the man on the central cross. Our Lord's prayer of forgiveness meant no more to that thief than the flight of a bird.

He saw no more purpose in his suffering than a fly sees purpose in the window pane that floods man's habitation with God's warmth and sunlight. Because he could not assimilate his pain and make it turn to the nourishment of his soul, pain turned against him as a foreign substance taken into the stomach turns against it and infects and poisons the whole system.

That is why he became bitter, why his mouth became like a crater of hate, and why he cursed the very Lord Who could have shepherded him into peace and paradise.

The world today is full of those who, like the thief on the left, see no meaning in pain. Knowing nothing of the redemption of Our Lord, they are unable to fit pain into a pattern; it becomes just an odd patch on the crazy quilt of life. Life becomes so wholly unpredictable for them that "a troubled manhood follows their baffled youth."

Never having thought of God as anything more than a name, they are now unable to fit the stark realities of life into His divine plan. That is why so many who cease to believe in God become cynics, killing not only themselves but, in a certain sense, even the beauties of flowers and the faces of children for whom they refuse to live.

The lesson of the thief on the left is clear: pain of itself does not make us better; it is very apt to make us worse. No man was ever better simply because he had an earache. Unspiritualized suffering does not improve man; it degenerates him. The thief at the left is no better for his crucifixion: it sears him, burns him, and tarnishes his soul.

Refusing to think of pain as related to anything else, he ends by thinking only of himself and who would take him down from the cross. So it is with those who have lost their faith in God. To them Our Lord on a cross is only an event in the history of the Roman Empire; He is not a message of hope or a proof of love.

They would not have a tool in their hands five minutes without discovering its purpose, but they live their lives without ever having inquired its meaning. Because they have no reason for living, suffering embitters them, poisons them, and finally, the great door of life's opportunity is closed in their faces, and like the thief on the left they go out into the night unblessed.

Now look at the thief on the right—the symbol of those for whom pain has a meaning. At first he did not understand it, and therefore joined in the curses with the thief on the left. But just as sometimes a flash of lightning will illumine the path we have missed, so too the Savior's forgiveness of His executioners illumined for the thief the road of mercy.

He began to see that if pain had no reason Jesus would not have embraced it. If the Cross had no purpose Jesus would not have climbed it. Surely He Who claimed to be God would never have taken that badge of shame unless it could be transformed and transmuted to some holy purpose.

Pain was beginning to be comprehensible to the thief; for the present at least it meant an occasion to do penance for his life of crime. And the moment that that light came to him he rebuked the thief on the left saying: "Neither dost thou fear God, seeing thou art under the same condemnation? And we indeed suffer justly, for we receive the due reward of our deeds; but this man hath done no evil" (Lk 23:40–41).

Now he saw pain as doing to his soul like to that which fire does to gold: burning away the dross. Or something like that which fever does to disease: killing the germs. Pain was dropping scales away from his eyes; and, turning toward the central cross, he no longer saw a crucified man, but a heavenly King.

Surely, He Who can pray for pardon for His murderers will not cast off a thief: "Lord, remember me when Thou shalt come into Thy kingdom." Such great faith found its reward: "Amen I say to thee, this day thou shalt be with Me in paradise" (Lk 23:42–43).

Pain in itself is not unbearable; it is the failure to understand its meaning that is unbearable. If that thief did not see purpose in pain, he would never have saved his soul. Pain can be the death of our soul, or it can be its life.

It all depends on whether or not we link it up with Him Who, "having joy set before him, endured the Cross". One of the greatest tragedies in the world is wasted pain. Pain without relation to the Cross is like an unsigned check—without value. But once we have it countersigned with the signature of the Savior on the Cross, it takes on an infinite value.

A feverish brow that never throbs in unison with a head crowned with thorns, or an aching hand never borne in patience with a hand on the Cross, is sheer waste. The world is worse for that pain when it might have been so much the better.

All the sickbeds in the world, therefore, are either on the right side of the Cross or on the left; their position is determined by whether, like the thief on the left, they ask to be taken down, or, like the thief on the right, they ask to be taken up.

It is not so much what people suffer that makes the world mysterious; it is rather how much they miss when they suffer. They seem to forget that even as children they made obstacles in their games in order to have something to overcome.

Why, then, when they grow into man's estate, should there not be prizes won by effort and struggle? Cannot the spirit of man rise with adversity as the bird rises against the resistance of the wind? Do not the game fish swim upstream? Must not the alabaster box be broken to fill the house with ointment? Must not the chisel cut away the marble to bring out the form? Must not the seed falling to the ground die before it can spring forth into life? Must not the little streams speed into the ocean to escape their stagnant self-content? Must not grapes be crushed that there may be wine to drink, and wheat ground that there may be bread to eat?

Why then cannot pain be made redemption? Why under the alchemy of divine love cannot crosses be turned into crucifixes? Why cannot chastisements be regarded as penances? Why cannot we use a cross to become God-like? We cannot become like Him in His power: we cannot become like Him in His knowledge.

There is only one way we can become like Him, and that is in the way He bore His sorrows and His Cross. And that way was with love. "Greater love than this no man hath, that a man lay down his life for his friends." It is love that makes pain bearable.

As long as we feel it is doing good for another, or even for our own soul by increasing the glory of God, it is easier to bear. A mother keeps a vigil at the bedside of her sick child. The world calls it "fatigue" but she calls it love.

A little child was commanded by his mother not to walk the picket fence. He disobeyed and fell, maimed himself and was never able to walk again. Being told of his misfortune he said to his mother: "I know I will never walk again; I know it is my own fault, but if you will go on loving me I can stand anything." So it is with our own pains.

If we can be assured that God still loves and cares, then we shall find joy even in carrying on His redemptive work—by being redeemers with a small "r" as He is Redeemer with a capital "R". Then will come to us the vision of the difference between pain and sacrifice. Pain is sacrifice without love. Sacrifice is pain with love.

When we understand this, then we shall have an answer for those who feel that God should have let us sin without pain:

> The cry of earth's anguish went up unto God,—
> "Lord, take away pain,—
> The shadow that darkens the world Thou hast made,
> The close-coiling chain
> That strangles the heart, the burden that weighs
> On the wings that would soar,—
> Lord, take away pain from the world Thou hast made
> That it love Thee the more."
>
> Then answered the Lord to the world He had
> made,
> "Shall I take away pain?
> And with it the power of the soul to endure
> Made strong by the strain?
> Shall I take away pity that knits heart to heart
> And sacrifice high?
> Will ye lose all your heroes who lift from the flame
> White brows to the sky?
> Shall I take away love that redeems with a price
> And smiles through the loss,—
> Can ye spare from the lives that would climb unto
> mine
> The Christ on His Cross?"[1]

You and I often ask God for many favors which are never granted. We can imagine the thief on the right during his life asking God for many favors, and very especially for wealth which was probably not granted. On the

[1] George Stewart, *God and Pain* (New York: George H. Doran, 1927).

other hand, though God does not always grant our material favors, there is one prayer He always grants.

There is a favor that you and I can ask of God this very moment, if we have the courage to do it, and that favor would be granted before the day is over. That prayer which God has never refused and will never refuse is the prayer for suffering. Ask Him to send you a cross and you will receive it!

But why does He not always answer our prayers for an increase in salary, for larger commissions, for more money? Why did He not answer the prayer of the thief on the left to be taken down from the cross, and why did He answer the prayer of the thief on the right to forgive his sins?

Because material favors draw us away from Him, but the Cross always draws us to Him—and God does not want the world to have us!

He wants us Himself because He died for us!

Why do the innocent suffer? We do not mean the innocent who have suffering involuntarily thrust upon them, but rather those good souls who go out in search of suffering and are impatient until they find a cross. In other words, why should there be Carmelites, Poor Clares, Trappists, Little Sisters of the Poor, and dozens of penitential orders of the Church, who do nothing but sacrifice and suffer for the sins of men?

Certainly not because suffering is necessarily connected with personal sin. Our Lord told us that much, when to those who asked concerning a blind boy, "Who hath sinned, this man, or his parents ...?" Our Lord answered "Neither."

If we are to find the answer we must go not merely to the suffering of innocent people, but to the suffering of innocence itself. Our attention is fixed—riveted upon the two most sinless creatures who ever trod our sinful earth: Jesus and Mary.

Jesus Himself was sinless by nature, for He is the all holy Son of God. Mary was sinless by grace, for she is "our tainted nature's solitary boast". And yet both suffer in the extreme. Why did He suffer Who had the power of God to escape the Cross? Why did she suffer who could have dispensed herself because of her virtue, or could have been excused by her Divine Son?

Love is the key to the mystery. Love by its very nature is not selfish, but generous. It seeks not its own, but the good of others. The measure of love is not the pleasure it gives—that is the way the world judges it—but the joy and peace it can purchase for others.

It counts not the wine it drinks, but the wine it serves. Love is not a circle circumscribed by self; it is a cross with arms embracing all mankind. It thinks not of having, but of being had, not of possessing but of being possessed, not of owning but of being owned.

Love then by its nature is social. Its greatest happiness is to gird its loins and serve the banquet of life. Its greatest unhappiness is to be denied the joy of sacrifice for others. *That is why in the face of pain, love seeks to unburden the sufferer and take his pain, and that is why in the face of sin, love seeks to atone for the injustice of him who sinned.*

Because mothers love, do they not want to take the pain of their children's wounds? Because fathers love, do they not take over the debts of wayward sons to expiate their foolishness?

What does all this mean but the "otherness" of love? In fact love is so social it would reject emancipation from pain, if the emancipation were for itself alone. Love refuses to accept individual salvation; it never bends over man, as the healthy over the sick, but enters into him to take his very sickness.

It refuses to have its eyes clear when other eyes are bedewed with tears; it cannot be happy unless everyone is happy, or unless justice is served; it shrinks from isolation and aloofness from the burdens and hungers of others. It spurns insulation from the shock of the world's sorrow, but insinuates itself into them, as if the sorrow were its very own.

This is not difficult to understand. Would you want to be the only person in all the world who had eyes to see? Would you want to be the only one who could walk in a universe of the lame? Would you, if you loved your family, stand on the dock and watch them all drown before your very eyes?

And if not, why not? Very simply, because you love them, because you feel so much one with them that their heartaches are your own heartbreaks. Now apply this to Our Lord and His Blessed Mother. Here is love at its peak, and innocence at its best.

Can they be indifferent to that which is a greater evil than pain, namely, sin? Can they watch humanity carry a cross to the Golgotha of death, while they themselves refuse to share its weight? Can they be indifferent to the outcome of love if they themselves *are* Love? If love means identification and sympathy with the one loved, then why should not God so love the world as to send His only-begotten Son into it to redeem the world? And if that Divine Son loved the world enough to die for it, why should not the Mother of love incarnate share that redemption? If human love identifies itself with the pain of the one loved, why should not divine love suffer when it comes in contact with sin in man? If mothers suffer in their children, if a husband grieves in the sorrow of his wife, and if friends feel the agony of their beloved's cross, why should not Jesus and Mary suffer in the humanity they love?

If you would die for your family of which you are the head, why should not He die for humanity of which He is the head? And if the deeper the love the more poignant the pain, why should not the Crucifixion be born of that love?

If a sensitive nerve is touched, it registers pain in the brain; and since Our Lord is the head of suffering humanity, He felt every sin of every man as His own. That is why the Cross was inevitable.

He could not love us perfectly unless He died for us. And His Mother could not love Him perfectly, unless she shared that death. That is why His life was given for us, and her heart broken for us; and that, too, is why He is Redeemer and she is Redemptrix—because they love.

In order more completely to reveal that a Cross was made up of the juncture of love and sin, Our Lord spoke His Third Word from the Cross to His Mother: "Woman, behold thy son"! He did not call her "mother" but "woman"; except when addressing John the next moment He added: "[Son] Behold thy Mother."

The term "woman" indicated a wider relationship to all mankind than "mother". It meant that she was to be not only His Mother, but that she was also to be the Mother of all men, as He was the Savior of all men. She was now to have many children—not according to the flesh, but according to the spirit. Jesus was her firstborn of the flesh in joy; John was her second-born of the spirit in sorrow; and we her millionth-and-millionth-born.

If she loved Him Who died for all men, then she must love those for whom He died. That was His clear, unmistakable meaning. The love of neighbor is inseparable from the love of God. His love had no limits; He died for every man. Her love then must have no limits.

It must not be merely unselfish; it must even be social. She must be the Mother of every man. An earthly mother loves her own children most, but Jesus is now telling her that even John is her son, too, and John was the symbol of all of us.

The Father did not spare His Son, nor did the Son spare His Mother, for love knows no bounds. Jesus had a sense of responsibility for every soul in the world; Mary, too, inspired by His love, had a corresponding sense of responsibility. If He would be the Redeemer of the wayward children, she must be their Mother.

Now does that throw any light on the problem? Why do innocent, pure, good souls leave the world and its pleasures, feast on fasts, embrace the Cross, and pray their hearts out? The answer is, *because they love.* "Greater love than this no man hath, that a man lay down his life for his friends."

They love the world so much that they want to save it, and they know there is no other way to save it, than to die for it. Many of us so love the world that we live *in* it and are *of* it, but in the end do nothing *for* it. Wrong indeed are they who say these innocent victims hate the world.

As soon as the world hears of a beautiful young woman or an upright young man entering the religious life, it asks: "Why did they leave the world?" They left the world, not because they hated the world, but because they loved it. They love the world with its human souls so much that they want to do all they can for it; and they can do nothing better for it than to pray that souls may one day find their way back to God.

Our Lord did not hate the world; it hated Him. But He loved it. Neither do they hate the world; they are in love with it and everyone in it. They so much love the sinners in it, that they expiate for their sins; they so much love the Communists in it, that they bless them as they send them to their God; they so much love the atheists in it, that they are willing to surrender the joy of the divine presence that the atheist may feel less afraid in the dark.

They are so much lovers of the world that they may be said to be organic with it. They know that things and souls are so much interrelated that the good which one does has repercussion on the millions, just as ten just men could have saved Sodom and Gomorrah. If a stone is thrown into the sea, it causes a ripple which widens in ever greater circles until it affects even the most distant shore; a rattle dropped from a baby's crib affects even the most distant star; a finger is burned and the whole body feels the pain.

The cosmos then is organic; but so also is mankind. We are all called to be members of a great family.

God is Our Father, Who sent His Son into the world to be Our Brother, and He on the Cross asked Mary to be our Mother. Now if in the human body it is possible to graft skin from one member to another, why is it not possible also to graft prayer?

If it is possible to transfuse blood, why is it not possible also to transfuse sacrifice? Why cannot the innocent atone for the sinful?

Why cannot the real lovers of souls, who refuse to be emancipated from sorrow, do for the world what Jesus did on the Cross and Mary did beneath it? The answer to this question has filled the cloisters.

No one on earth can measure the good these divine lovers are doing for the world. How often have they stayed the wrath of a righteous God! How many sinners have they brought to the confessional! How many deathbed conversions have they effected! How many persecutions have they averted!

We do not know, and they do not want to know, so long as love wins over hate. But let us not be foolish and ask: What good do they do for the world? We might as well ask: What good did the Cross do?

After all, only the innocent can understand what sin is. No one until the time of Our Lord ever thought of giving his life to save sinners, simply because no one was sinless enough to know its horrors.

We who have familiarized ourselves with it, become used to it, as a leprous patient after many years of suffering cannot wholly appreciate the danger of leprosy.

Sin has lost its horror; we never think of correlating it to the Cross: we never advert to its repercussions on mankind.

> Vice is a monster of so frightful mien,
> As to be hated, needs but to be seen;
> Yet seen too oft, familiar with her face,
> We first endure, then pity, then embrace.
>
> —Alexander Pope

The best way to know sin is by not sinning. But Jesus and Mary were wholly innocent—He by nature, she by grace; therefore they could understand and know the evil of sin.

Because they never compromised with it, there were now no compromises to be made. It was something so awful that to avoid it or to atone for it, they shrink not even from a death on the Cross.

But by a peculiar paradox, though innocence hates sin, because it alone knows its gravity, it nevertheless loves the sinner. Jesus loved Peter who fell three times, and Mary

chose as her companion at the foot of the Cross, a converted prostitute.

What must the scandalmongers have said of that friendship as they watched Mary and Magdalen ascend and
descend the hill of Calvary! But Mary braved it all, in
order that in a future generation you and I might have
hope in her as the "Refuge of Sinners". Let there be no
fear that she cannot understand our sinful misery because
she is immaculate, for if she had Magdalen as a companion
then, why can she not have us now?

11

Our Final Choice

There comes a time in the life of every man when at the supreme and tragic hour of death his friends and relatives ask, "How much did he leave?" It is just at that split second God is asking, "How much did he take with him?" It is only the latter question that matters, for it is only our works that follow us. The story of life is brief: "It is appointed unto men once to die and after this the judgment", for "the Son of Man shall come in the glory of His Father with His angels, and then will He render to every man according to his works." In the general forgetfulness of the Christian religion, which has passed over our civilization like a foul miasma, this great truth that a judgment follows death has been ignored in the moral outlook of the universe. Our souls can profit much from meditation upon it and its two important features; namely, its necessity and its nature.

All nature testifies to the necessity of judgment. Everywhere below man nature reveals itself as passing sentence on those who refuse to obey her laws. We need only look around us in the hospitals, prisons, and asylums to see that nature, like a judge seated in judgment, is squaring her accounts with those who violate her laws. If the body has abused itself by excess, nature takes revenge and passes the judgment of disease and infirmity. If a fragment of a star breaks from its central core and swings out of its orbit, nature passes the judgment that it shall burn itself out in space.

Nature settles her account with natural things here and now. But the moral side of the universe has not made its lasting reckoning with every man on this side of the grave: there is too much anguished innocence; too much unpunished wrong; too much suffering of the good; too much prosperity of the evil; too much pain for those who obey God's laws; too much pleasure for those who disobey them; too much good repute for those who sin unseen; too much scorn for those who pray unseen; too many unsung saints; too many glorified sinners; too many Pilates who act as righteous judges; too many Christs who go down to crucifixion; too many proud and vain souls who say, "I have sinned and nothing has happened."

But the reckoning day must come, and just as once a year each business man must balance his accounts, so too that important hour must come when every soul must balance its accounts before God. For life is like a cash register, in that every account, every thought, every deed, like every sale, is registered and recorded. And when the business of life is finally done, then God pulls from out the registry of our souls that slip of our memory on which is recorded our merits and demerits, our virtues and our vices—the basis of the judgment on which shall be decided eternal life or eternal death. We may falsify our accounts until that Day of Judgment, for God permits the wheat and the cockle to grow unto the harvest, but then, "in the time of the harvest, I will say to the reaper: gather up first the cockle and bind it into bundles to burn, but the wheat gather ye into my barn."

But what is the nature of judgment? In answer to this question we are more concerned with the particular judgment at the moment of death, than with the general judgment when all nations of the earth stand before their God. Judgment is a recognition both on the part of God and on the part of the soul.

First of all, it is a recognition on the part of God. Imagine two souls appearing before the sight of God, one in the state of grace, the other in the state of sin. Grace is a participation in the nature and life of God. Just as a man participates in the nature and life of his parents by being born of his parents, so too a man who is born of the Spirit of God by Baptism participates in the nature of God—the life of God, as it were, flows through his veins, imprinting an unseen but genuine likeness. When, therefore, God looks upon a soul in the state of grace, He sees in it a likeness of His own nature. Just as a father recognizes his own son because of likeness of nature, so too Christ recognizes the soul in the state of grace in virtue of resemblance to Him, and says to the soul: "Come ye blessed of My Father: I am the natural Son, you are the adopted son. Come into the Kingdom prepared for you from all eternity."

God looks into the other soul that is in the state of sin and has not that likeness, and just as a father knows his neighbor's son is not his own, so too God, looking at the sinful soul and failing to see therein the likeness of His own flesh and blood, does not recognize it as His own kind, and says to it as He said in the parable of the bridegroom, "I know you not"—and it is a terrible thing not to be known by God.

Not only is sin a recognition from God's point of view, but it is also a recognition from man's point of view. Just suppose that, while you were cleaning your car or your house, a very distinguished person was announced at the door. You would probably act differently than if you were thoroughly clean, well dressed, and presentable. In such an unclean condition you would ask to be excused, saying you were not fit to appear in the sight of such a person. When a soul is before the sight of God, it acts in much the same manner. Standing before the tremendous majestic presence of Almighty God, it does not plead, it does not argue, it does not entreat, it does not demand a second hearing, it does not protest the judgment, for it sees itself as it really is. In a certain sense, it judges itself, God merely sealing the judgment. If it sees itself clean and alive with the life of God, it runs to the embrace of love, which is heaven, just as a bird released from its cage soars into the skies. If it sees itself slightly stained and the robes of its Baptism remediably soiled, it protests that it is not to enter into the sight of purity, and hence throws itself into the purifying flames of purgatory. If it sees itself irremediably vitiated, having no likeness whatever to the purity and holiness of God; if it has lost all affection for the things of spirit, then it could no more endure the presence of God than a man who abhors beauty could endure the pleasure of music, art, and poetry. Why, heaven would be hell to such a soul, for it would be as much out of place in the holiness of heaven as a fish out of water. Hence, recognizing its own unworthiness, its own unholiness, its own ungodliness, its own distaste for the purity of God, it casts itself into hell in the same way that a stone, released from the hand, falls to the ground. Only three states, therefore, are possible after the particular judgment: heaven, purgatory, and hell. Heaven is love without pain, purgatory is pain with love; hell is pain without love.

There is one word which to modern ears probably signifies the unreal, the fictional, and even the absurd in the Christian vision of life, and that is the word "purgatory". Although the Christian world believed in it for sixteen centuries, for the last three hundred years it has ceased to be a belief outside the Church, and it has been regarded as a mere product of the imagination, rather than as a fruit of sound reason and inspiration. It is quite true to say that the belief in purgatory has declined in just the proportion that the modern mind has forgotten the two most important things in the world: the purity of God and the heinousness of sin. Once both of these vital beliefs are admitted, the doctrine of purgatory is unescapable. For what is purgatory but a place or condition of temporal punishment for those who depart this life in God's grace, but are not entirely free from venial faults or have not entirely paid the satisfaction due to their transgressions? Purgatory is that place in which the love of God tempers the justice of God, and secondly, where the love of man tempers the injustice of man.

First, purgatory is where the love of God tempers the justice of God. The necessity of purgatory is grounded upon the absolute purity of God. In the Book of Revelation we read of the great beauty of His city, of the pure gold, with its walls of jasper and its spotless light which is not of the sun nor the moon but the light of the Lamb slain from the beginning of the world. We also learn of the condition of entering the gates of that heavenly Jerusalem: "There shall not enter into it anything defiled, or that worketh abomination, or maketh a lie, but they that are written in the book of the life of the Lamb." Justice demands that nothing unclean, but only the pure of heart shall stand before the face of a pure God. If there were no purgatory, then the justice of God would be too terrible for words, for who are they who would dare assert themselves pure enough and spotless enough to stand before the immaculate Lamb of God? The martyrs who sprinkled the sands of the Coliseum with their blood in testimony of their faith? Most certainly! The missionaries like Paul who spend themselves and are spent for the spread of the gospel? Most assuredly! The cloistered saints who in the quiet calm of a voluntary Calvary become martyrs without recognition? Most truly! But these are glorious exceptions. How many millions there are who die with their souls stained with venial sin, who have known evil, and by their strong resolve have drawn from it only to carry with them the weakness of their past as a leaden weight.

The day we were baptized, the Church laid upon us a white garment with the injunction: "Receive this white garment which mayest thou carry without stain before the judgment seat of Our Lord Jesus Christ that thou mayest have life everlasting." How many of us during life have kept that garment unspotted and unsoiled by sin so that we might enter immediately upon death into the white-robed army of the King? How many souls departing this life have the courage to say that they left it without any undue attachment to creatures and that they were never guilty of a wasted talent, a slight cupidity, an uncharitable deed, a neglect of holy inspiration, or even an idle word for which every one of us must render an account? How many souls there are gathered in at the deathbed, like late-season flowers, that are absolved from sins, but not from the debt of their sins? Take any of our national heroes, whose names we venerate and whose deeds we emulate. Would any Englishman or American who knew something of the purity of God, as much as he loves and respects the virtues of a Lord Nelson or a George Washington, really believe that either of them at death were free enough from slight faults to enter immediately into the presence of God? Why the very nationalism of a Nelson or a Washington, which made them both heroes in war, might in a way make them suspect of being unsuited the second after death for that true internationalism of heaven, where there is neither

English nor American, Jew nor Greek, barbarian nor free, but all one in Christ Jesus Our Lord.

All these souls who die with some love of God possessing them are beautiful souls, but if there be no purgatory then because of their slight imperfections they must be rejected without pity by divine justice. Take away purgatory, and God could not pardon so easily, for will an act of contrition at the edge of the tomb atone for thirty years of sinning? Take away purgatory and the infinite justice of God would have to reject from heaven those who resolve to pay their debts, but have not yet paid the last farthing. Purgatory is where the love of God tempers the justice of God, for there God pardons because He has time to retouch these souls with His Cross, to recut them with the chisel of suffering, that they might fit into the great spiritual edifice of the heavenly Jerusalem, to plunge them into that purifying place where they might wash their stained baptismal robes to be fit to enter into the spotless purity of heaven; to resurrect them like the phoenix of old from the ashes of their own sufferings so that, like wounded eagles healed by the magic touch of God's cleansing flames, they might mount heavenward to the city of the pure where Christ is King and Mary is Queen, for, regardless of how trivial the fault, God cannot pardon without tears, and there are no tears in heaven.

Most men and women are quite unconscious of the injustice, the ingratitude, and the thanklessness of their lives until the cold hand of death is laid upon one they love. It is then, and only then, that they realize (and oh, with what regret!) the haunting poverty of their love and kindness. One of the reasons why the bitterest of tears are shed over graves is because of words left unsaid and deeds left undone. "The child never knew how much I loved her." "He never knew how much he meant to me." "I never knew how dear he was until he was gone." Such words are the poisoned arrows which cruel death shoots at our hearts from the door of every sepulcher. Oh, then we realize how differently we would act if only the departed one could come back again. Tears are shed in vain before eyes which cannot see; caresses are offered without response to arms that cannot embrace, and sighs stir not a heart whose ear is deaf. Oh, then the anguish for not offering the flowers before death had come and for not sprinkling the incense while the beloved was still alive and for not speaking the kind words that now must die on the very air they cleave. Oh, the sorrow at the thought that we cannot atone for the stinted affection we gave them, for the light answers we returned to their pleading, and for the lack of reverence we showed to one who was perhaps the dearest thing that God had ever given us to know. Alas, too late! It does little good to water last year's crop, to snare the bird that has flown, or to gather the rose that has withered and died.

Purgatory is a place where the love of God tempers the justice of God, but also where the love of man tempers the injustice of man, for it enables hearts who are left behind to break the barriers of time and death, to convert unspoken words into prayers, unburned incense into sacrifice, unoffered flowers into alms, and undone acts of kindness into help for eternal life. Take away purgatory and how bitter would be our grief for our unkindnesses and how piercing our sorrow for our forgetfulness. Take away purgatory and how meaningless are our Memorial Day and Armistice Day, when we venerate the memory of our dead. Take away purgatory and how empty are our wreaths, our bowed heads, our moments of silence. But, if there be a purgatory, then immediately the bowed head gives way to the bent knee, the moment of silence to a moment of prayer, and the fading wreath to the abiding offering of the sacrifice of that great hero of heroes, Christ.

Purgatory, then, enables us to atone for our ingratitude because, through our prayers, mortifications, and sacrifices, it makes it possible to bring joy and consolation to the ones we love. Love is stronger than death and hence there should be love for those who have gone before us. We are the offspring of their life, the gathered fruit of their labor, the solicitude of their hearts. Shall death cut off our gratitude, shall the grave stop our love, shall the cold clod prevent the atoning of our ingratitude? The Church assures us that not being able to give more to them in this world, since they are not of it, we can still seek them out in the hands of divine justice and give them the assurance of our love, and the purchasing price of their redemption.

Just as the man who dies in debt has the maledictions of his creditors following him to the grave, but may have his good name respected and revered by the labor of his son who pays the last penny, so too the soul of a friend who has gone to death owing a debt of penance to God may have it remitted by us who are left behind, by minting the gold of daily actions in the spiritual coin which purchases redemption. Into the crucibles of God these departed souls go like stained gold to have their dross burned away by the flames of love. These souls, who have not died in enmity with God, but have fallen wounded on the battlefield of life fighting for the victory of His cause, have not the strength to bind their own wounds and heal their own scars: it remains for us who are still strong and healthy, clad with the armor of faith and the shield of salvation, to heal their wounds and make them whole that they might join the ranks of the victors and march in the procession of the conquerors. We may be sure that if the penny that gives bread to the hungry body delivers a soul to the table of Our Lord, it will never forget us when it enters into the homeland of victory.

While yet confined to that prison of purifying fire, they hear the voices of the angels and saints who call them to their true fatherland, but they are incapable of breaking their chains for their time of merit is passed. Certainly God cannot be unmindful of a wife who offers her merits to the captive soul of a husband waiting for his deliverance. Surely the mercy of God cannot be such that He should be deaf to the good works of a mother who offers them for the liberation of her offspring who are yet stained with the sins of the world. Surely God will not forbid such communication of the living with the dead, since the great act of redemption is founded on the reversibility of merits. Responsive, then, will we be to the plea not only of our relatives and friends but of that great mass of unarmed warriors of the Church suffering who are yet wearing the ragged remnants of sin, but who, in their anxiety of soul to be clothed in the royal robes fit for entrance into the palace of the King, cry out to our responsive hearts the plaintive and tender plea: "Have mercy on me, have mercy on me, at least you, my friends, for the hand of the Lord has touched me."

If there is any subject which is offensive to modern sentimentalists it is the subject of hell. Our generation clamors for what the poet has called "a soft dean, who never mentions hell to ears polite", and our unsouled age wants a Christianity watered so as to make the gospel of Christ nothing more than a gentle doctrine of good will, a social program of economic betterment, and a mild scheme of progressive idealism.

There are many reasons why the modern world has ceased to believe in hell, among which we may mention, first, a psychological reason. If a man has led a very wicked life, he does not want to be disturbed in his wrongdoings by harsh words about justice. His wish that there be no final punishment for his crimes thus becomes father to the thought that there is no such thing as hell. That is why the wicked man denies hell, whereas the saint never denies it, but only fears it.

Another reason for the denial of hell is that some minds confuse the crude imagery of poets and painters with the reality of the moral order behind the doctrine. Eternal realities are not always easy to portray in the symbols of time and space, but that is no reason why they should be denied by anyone, any more than the reality of America should be denied because it is sometimes symbolized by a woman bearing a flag of red, white, and blue.

A final reason is found in that the doctrine of hell has been isolated from the organic whole of Christian truths. Once it is separated from the doctrines of sin, freedom, virtue, redemption, and justice, it becomes absurd as an eye separated from the body. The justice of this reasoning is borne out in the fact that men become scandalized about hell when they cease to be scandalized about sin. The Church has never altered one single iota the belief in an eternal hell as taught by her founder, Our Lord and Savior, Jesus Christ. In adherence to His divine testimony, the Church teaches first that hell is a demand of justice, and second that hell is a demand of love.

First of all, once it is recognized that the moral order is grounded on justice, then retribution beyond the grave becomes a necessity. All peoples have held it morally intolerable that by the mere fact of dying a murderer or an impenitent wrongdoer should triumphantly escape justice. The same fate cannot lie in store for the persecutor and the martyr; Nero and Paul, the Judas and Christ. If there is a supreme good to which man can attain only by courageous effort, it must follow that the man who neglects to make that effort imperils his felicity. Once it is granted that eternal life is a thing which has to be won, then there must always be the grim possibility that it may also be lost.

Even the order of nature itself suggests retribution for every violation of a law. There is a physical law to the effect that for every action there is a contrary and equal reaction. If, for example, I stretch a rubber band three inches, it will react with a force equal to three inches. If I stretch it six inches, it will react with a force equal to six inches. If I stretch it twelve inches, it will react with a force equal to a foot. This physical law has its counterpart in the moral order, in which every sin necessarily implies punishment. What is sin but an action against a certain order? There are three orders against which a man may sin: first the order of individual conscience, second the order of the union of consciences, or the state, and third the source of both, or God. Now, if I sin or act against my conscience, there is a necessary reaction in the form of remorse of conscience which, in normal individuals, varies with the gravity of the sin committed. Secondly, if I act or sin against the union of consciences, or the state, there is a contrary and equal reaction which takes the form of a fine, imprisonment, or death sentence meted out by the state. It is worthy of note that the punishment is never determined by the length of time required to commit the crime, but rather by the nature of the crime itself. It takes only a second to commit murder, and yet the state may take away life for such an offense. Finally, whenever I sin against God, and this I do when I rebel either against the order of conscience or state, I am acting contrary to one who is infinite. For this action, there is bound to be a reaction. The reaction from the infinite must, therefore, be infinite, and an infinite reaction from God is an infinite separation from God, and an

infinite separation from God is an eternal divorce from life
and truth and love, and an eternal divorce from life and
truth and love is—*hell!*

It should be evident, therefore, that eternal punishment is not an arbitrary construction of theologians but
is the very counterpart of sin. We are too often wont to
look upon hell as an afterthought in the mind of God and
regard it as related to sin in the same way that a spanking
is related to an act of disobedience on the part of a child.
This is not true. The punishment of spanking is something
which does not necessarily follow upon an act of disobedience. It may be a consequence, but it need not be. Rather
it is true to say that hell is related to a sinful and evil life
in the same way that blindness is related to the plucking
out of an eye, for the two are inseparable. One necessarily
follows the other. Life is a harvest and we reap what we
sow: if we sow in sin, we reap corruption; but if we sow
in the spirit, we reap life everlasting.

The teaching of Our Blessed Lord bears out this
demand of justice, for His doctrine was not merely an
amiable gospel of indifference as His own life was not one
of sentimental good-naturedness. He very distinctly taught
that men might do things which would prove their undoing. Never did He give assurance that He would succeed
with everyone. The very fact that He poured out His life's
blood to redeem us from sin could only mean that sin
might have such a terrible consequence as hell. For, on
the Last Day, the good shall be separated from the bad,
and the sheep from the goats. Then "shall the King say to
them that shall be on His right hand: 'Come, ye blessed
of My Father, possess you the kingdom prepared for you
from the foundation of the world. For I was hungry, and
you gave Me to eat: I was thirsty, and you gave Me drink:
I was a stranger, and you took Me in.... Amen, I say to

you, as long as you did it to one of these My least brethren, you did it to Me.' Then He shall say to them also that shall be on His left hand: 'Depart from Me, you cursed, into everlasting fire which was prepared for the devil and his angels. For I was hungry, and you gave Me not to eat: I was thirsty, and you gave Me not to drink: I was a stranger, and you took Me not in.... As long as you did it not to one of these least, neither did you do it to Me.' And these shall go into everlasting punishment: but the just, into life everlasting." These are the words of the Son of God Who is truth itself, and it is difficult to understand why anyone, knowing and admitting this, should accept His words concerning heaven, and deny His words concerning hell. If He is worthy of belief in one instance, He must be worthy of belief in another.

Hell is not only demanded by justice, but also by love. The failure to look upon hell as involving love makes men ask the question, "How can a God of love create a place of everlasting punishment?" This is like asking why a God of love should be a God of justice. It forgets that the sun which warms so gently may also wither, and the rain which nourishes so tenderly may also rot. Those who cannot reconcile the God of love with hell do not know the meaning of love. There is nothing sweeter than love; there is nothing more bitter than love; there is nothing which so much unites souls and so much separates them as love. Love demands reciprocity; love seeks a lover; and when love finds reciprocity there is a fusion and a compenetration and a union to a sublime and ecstatic degree. And when it is a question of the love of God and the love of the soul, that is the happiness of heaven. But suppose that love does not find reciprocity; or suppose that love does find it only to be betrayed, spurned, and rejected. Can love still forgive? Love can forgive injuries and betrayals and insults, and divine love can forgive even to seventy times seven. But there is only one thing in the world which human love cannot forgive, and there is only one thing in eternity which divine love cannot forgive, and that is the refusal of love. When, therefore, the soul by a final free act refuses to return human love for divine love, then divine love abandons it to its own selfishness, to its own solitariness, to its own loneliness. And what punishment in all the world is comparable to being abandoned, not by the lovely but by the love which is God?

Love forgives everything except one thing, and that is the refusal to love. A human heart pursues another and sues for its affection with all the purity and high ardor of its being. It showers the loved one with gifts, tokens of sacrifice, and all the while remains most worthy of a responding affection. However, if, after a long and weary pursuit, it has been not only spurned and rejected but betrayed, that human heart turns away and bursting with a pent-up emotion in obedience to the law of love, cries out: "Love has done all that it can. I can forgive anything except the refusal to love."

Something of this kind takes place in the spiritual order. God is the great lover on the quest of His spouse, which is the human soul. He showers it with gifts, admits it into His royal family in the Sacrament of Baptism, into His royal army in the Sacrament of Confirmation, and invites it to His royal table in the Sacrament of the Everlasting Bread, and countless times during human life whispers to it in health and sickness, in sorrow and joy, to respond to His plaintive pleadings, abandon a life of sin, and return love for love. If, however, the human heart, after rejecting this love many times only to be re-loved again, after ignoring the knock of Christ at the door of his soul only to hear the knock again, finally, at the moment of death completely spurns and rejects that divine goodness, then the God of love, in obedience to the law of love, cries out: "Love has done all that it can. I can forgive everything except the refusal to love." And it is a terrible thing to be through with love, for once divine love departs at death, it never returns: that is why hell is eternal!—that is why hell is a place where there is no love!

Time is the one thing that makes real pleasure impossible, for the simple reason that it does not permit us to make a club sandwich of pleasures. By its very nature, it forbids us to have many pleasures together under the penalty of having none of them at all. By the mere fact that I exist in time, it is impossible for me to combine the pleasures of marching with the old guard of Napoleon, and at the same time, advancing under the flying eagles of Caesar. By the mere fact that I live in time, I cannot enjoy simultaneously the winter sports of the Alps, and the limpid waters of the Riviera. Time makes it impossible for me to be stirred by the oratory of a Demosthenes, and at the same time to listen to the melodious accents of the great Bossuet. Time does not permit me to combine the prudence that comes with age and the buoyancy that belongs to youth. It is the one thing which prevents me from gathering around the same festive table with Aristotle, Socrates, Thomas Aquinas, and Mercier in order to learn the secrets of great minds in solving the riddles of a universe. If it were not for time, Dante and Shakespeare could have sipped tea together, and Homer even now might tell us his stories in English. It is all very nice and lovely to enjoy the mechanical perfections of this age of luxury, but there are moments when I would like to enjoy the calm and peace of the Middle Ages, but time will not permit it. If I live in the twentieth century, I must sacrifice the pleasures of the thirteenth, and if I enjoy the Athenian age of Pericles, I must be denied the Florentine age of Dante.

Thus it is that time makes it impossible to combine pleasures. I know there are advertisements which would invite us to dine and dance, but no one can do both comfortably at one and the same time. All things are good, and yet none can be enjoyed except in their season, and the enjoyment must always be tinged with the regret that time will demand their surrender. Time gives me things, but it also takes them away. When it does give, it gives but singly, and thus life becomes but "just one fool thing after another".

This thought suggests the suspicion that if time makes the combination of pleasures impossible, then if I could ever transcend time, I might, in some way, increase my happiness, and this I find to be true, for every conscious desire to prolong a pleasure is a desire to make it an enduring "now". Like cats before the fire, we want to prolong the pleasure indefinitely; we want it to be permanent and not successive.

Go back in the storehouse of your memory, and you will find ample proof that it is always in those moments when you are least conscious of the passing of time that you most thoroughly enjoy the pleasures of time. How often it happens, for example, when listening to an absorbing conversation or the thrilling experiences of a much traveled man, that the hours pass by so quickly we are hardly conscious of them, and we say, "The time passes like everything." What is true of a delightful conversation is also true of aesthetic pleasures. I dare say that very few would ever notice the passing of time listening to an orchestra translate the beauty of one of Beethoven's works. In just the proportion that it pleases and thrills, it makes us unconscious of how long we were absorbed by its melodies. The contrary fact illustrates the same truth. The more we notice time, the less we are being interested. If our friends keep looking at their watches while we tell a story, we can be very sure that they are being bored by our story. A man who keeps his eye on the clock is not the man who is interested in his work. The more we notice the passing of time, the less is our pleasure, and the less we notice the passing of time, the greater is our pleasure.

These psychological facts of experience testify that not only is time the obstacle of enjoyment, but escape from it is the essential of happiness. Suppose we could enlarge upon our experience in such a way as to imagine ourselves completely outside of time and succession, in a world where there would never be a "before" nor an "after", but only a "now". Suppose we could go out to another existence where the great pleasures of history would not be denied us because of their historical incompatibility, but all unified in a beautiful hierarchical order, like a pyramid in that all would minister to the very unity of our personality. Suppose I say that I could reach a point of timelessness at which all the enjoyments and beauties and happinesses of time could be reduced to those three fundamental unities which constitute the perfection of our being, namely, life and truth and love, for into these three all pleasures can be resolved.

Suppose first of all that I could reduce to a single focal point all the pleasures of life, so that in the now which never looked before nor after, I could enjoy the life that seems to be in the sea when its restless bosom is dimpled with calm, as well as the urge of life that seems to be in all the hill-encircling brooks that loiter to the sea; the life which provokes the dumb, dead sod to tell its thoughts in violets; the life which pulsates through a springtime blossom as the swinging cradle for the fruit; the life of the flowers as they open the chalice of their perfume to the sun; the life of the birds as the great heralds of song and messengers of joy; the life of all the children that run shouting to their mothers' arms; the life of all the parents that beget a life like unto their own; and the life of the mind that on the wings of an invisible thought strikes out to the hid battlements of eternity to the life whence all living comes. . . .

Suppose that in addition to concentrating all the life of the universe in a single point, I could also concentrate in another focal point all the truths of the world, so that I could know the truth the astronomer seeks as he looks up through his telescope, and the truth the biologist seeks as he looks down through his microscope; the truth about the heavens, and who shut up the sea with doors when it did burst forth as issuing from a womb; the truth about the hiding place of darkness and the treasure house of hail, and the cave of the winds; the truth about the common things: why fire, like a spirit, mounts to the heavens heavenly, and why gold, like clay, falls to the earth earthly; the truth the philosopher seeks as he tears apart with his mind the very wheels of the universe; the truth the theologian seeks as he uses Revelation to unravel the secrets of God which far surpass those that John heard as he leaned his head upon the breast of his Master. . . .

Suppose that over and above all these pleasures of life and truth, there could be unified in another focal point all the delights and beauties of love that have contributed to the happiness of the universe: the love of the patriot for his country; the love of the soldier for his cause; the love of the scientist for his discovery; the love of the flowers as they smile upon the sun; the love of the earth at whose breast all creation drinks the milk of life; the love of mothers, who swing open the great portals of life that a child may see the light of day; the love of friend for friend to whom he could reveal his heart through words; the love of spouse for spouse; the love of husband for wife; and even the love of angel for angel, and the angel for God with a fire and heat sufficient to enkindle the hearts of ten thousand times ten thousand worlds....

Suppose that all the pleasures of the world could be brought to these three focal points of life and truth and love, just as the rays of the sun are brought to unity in the sun; and suppose that all the successive pleasures of time could be enjoyed at one and the same now; and suppose that these points of unity on which our hearts and minds and souls would be directed, would not merely be three abstractions, but that the focal point in which all the pleasures of life were concentrated would be a life personal enough to be a Father, and that that focal point of truth in which all the pleasures of truth were concentrated, would not merely be an abstract truth personal enough to be a Word or a Son, and that that focal point of love in which all the pleasures of love were concentrated, would be not merely an abstract love, but a love personal enough to be a Holy Spirit; and suppose that once elevated to that supreme height, happiness would be so freed from limitations that it would include these three as one, not in succession, but with a permanence; not as in time, but as in the timeless—then we would have eternity, then we would have God! The Father, Son, and Holy Ghost: Perfect Life, Perfect Truth, Perfect Love. Then we would have happiness—and that would be heaven.

Will the pleasures of that timelessness with God and that enjoyment of life and truth and love which is the Trinity be in any way comparable to the pleasures of time? Is there anyone on this earth that will tell me about heaven? Certainly there are three faculties to which one might appeal, namely, to what one has seen, to what one has heard, and to what one can imagine. Will heaven surpass all the pleasures of the eye and the ear and the imagination? First of all, will it be as beautiful as some of the things that can be seen? I have seen the Villa d'Este of Rome with its long lanes of ilex and laurel, and its great avenues of cypress trees, all full of what might be called the vivacity of quiet and living silence; I have seen a sunset on the Mediterranean when two clouds came down like pillars to form a brilliant red tabernacle for the sun and it glowing like a golden host; I have seen, from the harbor, the towers and the minarets of Constantinople pierce through the mist which hung over them like a silken veil; I have seen the château country of France and her Gothic cathedrals aspiring heavenward like prayers; I have seen the beauties of the castles of the Rhine, and the combination of all these visions almost makes me think of the doorkeeper of the Temple of Diana who used to cry out to those who entered: "Take heed to your eye", and so I wonder if the things of eternity will be as beautiful as the combined beauty of all the things which I have seen....

I have not seen all the beauties of nature, others I have heard of that I have not seen: I have heard of the beauties of the hanging gardens of Babylon, of the pomp and dignity of the palaces of the Doges, of the brilliance and glitter of the Roman Forum as its foundations rocked with the tramp of Rome's resistless legions; I have heard of the splendor of the Temple of Jerusalem as it shone like a jewel in the morning sun; I have heard of the beauties of the Garden of Paradise where fourfold rivers flowed through lands rich with gold and onyx, a garden made beautiful as only God knows how to make a beautiful garden; I have heard of countless other beauties and joys of nature which tongue cannot describe, nor touch of brush convey, and

I wonder if all the joys and pleasures of heaven will be as great as the combined beauty of all the things of which I have heard. . . .

Beyond what I have heard and seen, there are things which I can imagine: I can imagine a world in which there never would be pain, nor disease, nor death; I can imagine a world wherein every man would live in a castle, and in that commonwealth of castles there would be a due order of justice without complaint or anxiety; I can imagine a world in which the winter would never come, and in which the flowers would never fade, and the sun would never set; I can imagine a world in which there would always be a peace and quiet without idleness, a profound knowledge of things without research, a constant enjoyment without satiety; I can imagine a world which would eliminate all the evils and diseases and worries of life, and combine all of its best joys and happiness, and I wonder if all the happiness of heaven would be like the happiness of earth which I can imagine. . . .

Will eternity be anything like what I have seen, or what I have heard, or what I can imagine? No, eternity will be nothing like anything I have seen, heard, or imagined. Listen to the voice of God: "Eye hath not seen, nor ear heard, neither hath it entered into the heart of man what things God hath prepared for them that love Him."

If the timeless so much surpasses time that there can be found no parallel for it, then I begin to understand the great mystery of the shape of the human heart. The human heart is not shaped like a valentine heart, perfect and regular in contour; it is slightly irregular in shape as if a small piece of it were missing out of its side. That missing part may very well symbolize a piece that a spear tore out of the universal heart of humanity on the Cross, but it probably symbolizes something more. It may very well mean that when God created each human heart, He kept a small sample of it in heaven, and sent the rest of it into the world of time where it would each day learn the lesson that it could never be really happy, never be really wholly in love, and never be really *whole*hearted until it went back again to the timeless to recover the sample which God had kept for it for all eternity.

ACKNOWLEDGMENTS

The author wishes to acknowledge with gratitude the courtesy of the following publishers, who have allowed him to reprint material from his earlier words.

From *The Life of All Living* by Fulton J. Sheen. Copyright 1929 by The Century Company. Reprinted by permission of the publishers, Appleton-Century-Crofts, Inc.

From *Moods and Truths* by Fulton J. Sheen. Copyright 1932 by The Century Company. Reprinted by permission of the publishers, Appleton-Century-Crofts, Inc.

From *Three to Get Married* by Fulton J. Sheen. Copyright 1951 by Fulton J. Sheen. Reprinted by permission of the publishers, Appleton-Century-Crofts, Inc.

From *Rock Plunged into Eternity* by Fulton J. Sheen, 1950. Reprinted by permission of the National Council of Catholic Men.

From *Rainbow of Sorrow* by Fulton J. Sheen. Copyright 1938 by P. J. Kenedy & Sons. Reprinted by permission of the publishers, P. J. Kenedy & Sons.

From *Preface to Religion* by Fulton J. Sheen. Copyright 1946 by P. J. Kenedy & Sons. Reprinted by permission of the publishers, P. J. Kenedy & Sons.

From *Way to Happiness* by Fulton J. Sheen. Copyright 1954 by Doubleday & Co. Copyright 1949, 1950, 1951, 1952, 1953 by the George Matthew Adams Service.